HOW TO LEAD A DISCIPLINED LIFE

A QUICKSTART GUIDE TO DEVELOPING SELF-DISCIPLINE, IMPROVING WILLPOWER, AND STRENGTHENING SELF-CONTROL

.

DAMON ZAHARIADES

ARTOFPRODUCTIVITY.COM

CONTENTS

Other Books by Damon Zahariades   v

Your Free Gift   1
Notable Quotables about Self-Discipline   3
Introduction   4
My Story   6
What You'll Learn in How to Lead a
Disciplined Life   14

PART I
PRINCIPLES OF SELF-DISCIPLINE

Self-Discipline Defined   19
Why Self-Discipline Is Important   26
Self-Discipline and Delayed Gratification   34
Self-Discipline During Times of Stress   42
Common Misconceptions About Self-
Discipline   48
Self-Discipline vs. Willpower   55
Self-Discipline vs. Motivation   61
Self-Discipline Stumbling Blocks   70

PART II
10 STEPS TO BUILDING SELF-DISCIPLINE

Step #1: Create Small, Purposeful,
Achievable Goals   85
Step #2: Develop A Method To Monitor
Your Progress   92
Step #3: Get Clear On Your Reason Why   99
Step #4: Learn to Manage Resistance   105
Step #5: Clarify Your Sacrifice   112
Step #6: Use the 10-10-10 Rule   119

Step #7: Embrace Discomfort Through
Training   127
Step #8: Turn Actions Into Systems   133
Step #9: Minimize and Manage Stressors   140
Step #10: Forgive Yourself When You
Stumble   148
BONUS STEP #1: Make Yourself
Accountable To Someone   154
BONUS STEP #2: Create A
Reward/Consequence System   160
BONUS STEP #3: Identify A Role Model   166
Your Self-Discipline Action Plan: A 60-
Second Recap   172

PART III
**HOW TO STAY DISCIPLINED FOR A
LIFETIME**

Creating Your Self-Discipline Habit   179
Reinforcing Your Self-Discipline Habit   185
Managing Your Self-Discipline Habit   191
The Effect of Lifestyle Choices on Your
Self-Discipline Habit   197

Final Thoughts on How to Lead a
Disciplined Life   203
Did You Enjoy Reading How to Lead a
Disciplined Life?   205

About the Author   207
Other Books by Damon Zahariades   209

OTHER BOOKS BY DAMON ZAHARIADES

~

The P.R.I.M.E.R. Goal Setting Method

Improve Your Focus and Mental Discipline series

Fast Focus

Morning Makeover

Digital Detox

Visit ArtofProductivity.com for a complete list of titles and summaries. All titles are available for purchase at ArtofProductivity.com/Amazon.

YOUR FREE GIFT

 ~

I want to give you a gift. It's my way of saying thanks for purchasing this book. It's my 40-page PDF action guide titled *Catapult Your Productivity! The Top 10 Habits You Must Develop to Get More Things Done.*

It's short enough to read quickly but meaty enough to offer actionable advice that can make a real difference in your life.

You can get immediate access to *Catapult Your Productivity* by clicking the link below and joining my mailing list:

http://artofproductivity.com/free-gift/

We're about to embark on a journey together. It won't be easy. We're going to encounter obstacles that will try to waylay us. But we have a map that shows us the way. We're going to follow this map carefully and closely.

Though this journey will occasionally be difficult, you'll (hopefully) find it rewarding and worthwhile. By the time we reach our destination, you'll possess everything you need to control your impulses and go beyond your limits when the situation requires.

So, let's gather our gear and set off.

NOTABLE QUOTABLES ABOUT SELF-DISCIPLINE

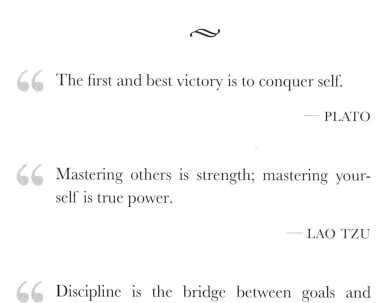

66 The first and best victory is to conquer self.

— PLATO

66 Mastering others is strength; mastering yourself is true power.

— LAO TZU

66 Discipline is the bridge between goals and accomplishment.

—JIM ROHN

INTRODUCTION

~

Think of the most disciplined person you know. They didn't start that way. They weren't born that way. No one is born disciplined. We are born *undisciplined*. From the beginning, we struggle with our weaknesses. We give in to them and let them run our lives.

Until we decide to let them no longer.

We resolve to fight against our nature. We lose a lot of battles. But we slowly learn temperance and self-control. We learn to rein in our impulses. We learn the value of self-restraint. And we begin to recognize the many rewards that this makes available to us.

Tasting victory, we press forward. With time and constantly renewed commitment, we start to lose fewer battles. We make incremental progress toward becoming self-disciplined.

We still experience failures, of course. We stumble. We lose minor skirmishes along the way. But we no longer feel as though we're fighting a losing battle. We're fighting a *winning* battle. The losses become less frequent. And while the war never truly ends — we must be vigilant because we're always at risk of falling back into laziness and bad habits — less effort is required to overcome our nature.

Eventually, after tremendous effort and relentless application (and perhaps a bit of heartache), we gain the upper hand over our impulses. We triumph.

This is the battle each of us wages to lead a disciplined life.

Damon Zahariades
Art of Productivity
September 2023

MY STORY

∾

I was raised in a household that emphasized self-discipline. Impulse control was praised. Laziness was discouraged. Temperance and moderation were commended. Overindulgence and excess were scorned.

To be clear, there was no shortage of affection and tenderness in my home when I was a child. I don't want to give the impression that my parents were autocratic. On the contrary, they showered my brother and me with the type of love, compassion, and encouragement that parents are uniquely capable of expressing toward their children.

Having said that, examining that period in my life brings a sober realization. I recognize now that my parents were imparting tough, valuable lessons to my brother and me regarding the many merits of self-discipline.

These lessons were often brushed aside. I was headstrong. Obstinate. Indolent. Sometimes unbridled (a charitable person might say "independent" or "free-spirited").

As expected, life imposed consequences.

The Early Years

I was overweight as a child. Like most children, I had a sweet tooth. I wasn't mature enough to restrain my impulses, so I ate as much junk food as possible. My parents made heroic attempts to limit my consumption, but I was often beyond their supervision between school, swim practice, and time spent with friends.

Despite being active and constantly burning calories, I gained weight.

I swam competitively from an early age (6 years old). As you can imagine, being overweight posed a problem for me. It hampered my performance. Despite dreams of becoming great, I rarely rose above good. By the time I entered high school, I was barely mediocre. It was clear that my days of swimming competitively were coming to an end.

I quit when I was 15.

Schoolwork presented another problem. Lacking discipline, I failed to study as much as I should have. It was only because of my mother's insistence that I put in the time and effort that I did so. Without her influence, I likely would have failed classes. Even then, I occasionally neglected to complete assignments and often did poorly on exams.

This problem began to rear its head in high school. I had more autonomy and more opportunity to squander time that should have been spent studying. I did reasonably well but never came close to matching the academic performance of more disciplined students.

It was time for me to apply to colleges during my senior year. I aspired to attend a prestigious institution. None accepted me. My grades weren't good enough. And I had few, if any, extracurricular activities to show. With my options limited, I attended a university that lacked the status and reputation of better schools.

College was an exciting time. I enjoyed more autonomy than ever. Unfortunately, this freedom did more harm than good. Presented with the choice to study or not, I regularly chose the latter. I lacked the foresight to anticipate how doing so would impact me.

In middle school and high school, total failure was unlikely. Homework was relatively simple. Exams were sometimes difficult but manageable with cramming. College was different. Assignments required a great deal of time and effort. Exams were often undoable without spending hours studying for them.

I was forced to drop at least one class and performed poorly in others. Moreover, I constantly fell asleep during lectures due to an erratic sleep schedule (consistent with leading an undisciplined life). One of my professors took me aside and asked if everyone was okay at home. He was concerned.

My lack of discipline and inability to control my

impulses would continue to impose costs in ways I regrettably failed to predict.

Out of School and Into the Workplace

I finished college and got a corporate job. Though I aspired to a position that promised a high salary and exposure to powerful and influential leaders, it was not to be. My academic performance in college proved to be a stumbling block. My transcripts were unimpressive, and the position I was offered was lower in the corporate food chain.

Much lower.

You'd think that I would've learned my lessons. You'd think I would've possessed the awareness to recognize my failings, acknowledge their ill effects, and make changes. But I didn't. Or, more accurately, I recognized my mistakes, but not in a way that compelled me to take responsibility for them. Not in a way that drove me to cultivate self-discipline.

I continued to give in to my impulses. I was self-indulgent, regularly prioritizing instant gratification over deferred rewards attached to time and effort invested in the present.

This affected my job performance, of course. The quality of my work suffered. Consequently, I was passed over for promotions and was given fewer opportunities to "shine." The effects of my lack of discipline were evident outside the workplace, too. I continued to struggle with my weight. My relationships suffered. I no longer had hobbies that required focus, time, and effort.

It was an empty time in my life. I rarely experienced the deep satisfaction that accompanies great achievements. I rarely enjoyed the emotional rewards that come with knowing one's toil has paid off in a measurable way.

I was unhappy. I felt purposeless. But rather than focusing inward and recognizing that these feelings might stem from my lack of discipline, I focused outward. I presumed that my despondency was due to my career. Instead of reflecting on whether this was true (reflection requires discipline), I convinced myself it was.

I decided to make a change.

I quit my job.

Embarking On My Own (The Bitter Taste of Failure)

While working in corporate America, I started a side business. After I quit my job, I devoted myself to building this business.

You might think that this required temperance and self-control. And to a point, it did. Side businesses don't build themselves. But remember, I hadn't yet recognized the adverse effects of my indiscipline. At the very least, I hadn't *owned* them. So, I continued to lead my "footloose and fancy-free" lifestyle.

For example, I'd play video games with friends without regard for the time. I'd regularly go to bed at 2:00 a.m., waking up at 5:00 a.m. and relying on coffee to fill the gap.

My diet was terrible, and my health suffered. My attention span eroded, and my relationships suffered. I continued to struggle with my weight. Though I enjoyed the freedom of not having a regular job, I continued to feel unhappy.

My side business grew and produced significant revenue, enough to distract from these failings. Something about running a successful business persuades you to take for granted that you're on the right path. I assumed (wrongly) that I was making good decisions. I figured (wrongly) that I was spending my time wisely.

These assumptions proved to be disastrous. My unmerited confidence camouflaged fundamental problems in my business.

Eventually, the business failed.

Progress Report

Everything is different today.

Following the failure of my business, I finally sat down and reflected on my life to that point. I want to say this was motivated by self-awareness and epiphany. But that's not true. It was motivated by despair, frustration, and stress. This sounds depressing, but it was the impetus I needed to identify the core issues underlying my failures.

I accepted some hard truths about myself. And I acknowledged that I needed to make substantive changes to experience a rewarding life.

I decided to work on my self-discipline. Ironically, before the failure of my business, I presumed that I *was* self-disciplined. It's remarkable (and alarming) how easy it was to delude myself — how quick I was to embrace this delusion. Once I confronted my shortcomings and accepted them (*owned* them), I saw that I truly had only one path to take. This path promised to involve a lot of work. But it also promised rewards that I deeply — even desperately — desired.

The decision changed my life.

Postscript

My life before deciding to become more disciplined wasn't just a string of failures. There were periods during which I experienced great success, joy, and satisfaction. But these periods were always limited, unreliable, or short-lived in some way.

For example, I lost weight but gained it back. I was promoted several times, but witnessed coworkers who performed better being promoted ahead of me. I enjoyed rewarding relationships, but most fizzled. There were many ups and downs.

Cultivating self-discipline allowed me to smooth the curve. Of course, there are still ups and downs, but the highs aren't so high, and the lows aren't so low. Instead, there's more consistency. Furthermore, much of the nonsense that led to the depressing, despairing lows of the past is gone.

Today, my health has dramatically improved. My weight is where I want it. My relationships are better and more rewarding. And my work (mostly writing) fills me with a much deeper sense of satisfaction and accomplishment.

If you've read this far, thank you. It's uncomfortable to reveal so many of my past failings and disappointments. I hope that my story shows the detrimental effects of being stubbornly undisciplined. You may even relate to some of it in your experiences.

The salient point of my story is that change is possible. Regardless of your circumstances, you can decide today to improve your impulse control, overcome laziness, and live in a manner that aligns with your values, convictions, and aspirations. To that end, I hope that you're inspired to lead a disciplined life.

WHAT YOU'LL LEARN IN HOW TO LEAD A DISCIPLINED LIFE

∾

This book is composed of three distinct parts. Each part has a singular purpose (which I'll detail below). They work together to form a personal workshop of sorts.

How to Lead a Disciplined Life is written with daily implementation in mind. Practical exercises follow actionable tips and strategies. The proposition of this book is simple: apply the tips and do the exercises, and I guarantee you'll develop discipline and self-control.

Here's a quick roadmap detailing what you'll find in *How to Lead a Disciplined Life*:

Part I

We'll lay the groundwork for developing self-discipline by investigating its main building blocks. One obstacle preventing people from improving this aspect of their lives is a feeling of overwhelm. This feeling stems from uncertainty regarding what self-discipline is.

In *Part I: Principles of Self-Discipline*, we define it precisely and discuss its importance. We'll explore its many facets related to how you can apply it in your life. By the time you finish reading *Part I*, you'll know everything you need to move forward toward mastering self-discipline confidently.

Part II

We'll set aside theory and instead focus on actionable steps you can take immediately. When developing any habit or personal attribute, nothing is as helpful and effective as a step-by-step action plan.

The rubber meets the road in *Part II: 10 Steps to Building Self-Discipline*. This is where the work begins, and actual progress is made. Each step in this section is explained in detail and followed by a simple exercise. The exercises are designed with two goals in mind:

1. demonstrate the concepts they accompany
2. help you apply and master them

Once you finish *Part II*, you'll have completed a

comprehensive, fast-track program for improving your impulse control, resisting temptations, and sticking to your goals, values, and convictions.

Part III

Self-discipline is like a muscle. Use it daily, and it becomes stronger. Fail to use it, and it'll decay. Once you develop self-discipline, you must regularly exercise it lest it deteriorate.

In *Part III: How to Stay Self-Disciplined for a Lifetime*, we'll explore several ways you can "stay in shape." You'll learn practical strategies you can use to ensure your decisions and behaviors consistently align with your intentions.

The Road Forward

We're going to move quickly through this material. Although each concept, tactic, and strategy is explained in-depth, no time will be wasted on matters that don't actively move us forward. I aim to help you reach the end of this book as quickly as possible while making as much headway as possible.

Are you ready to enjoy greater control over your desires and impulses? Are you eager to achieve your goals uninfluenced by laziness or your emotions in the moment? Would you like to take purposeful, consistent action every time you decide to do something?

If so, let's roll up our sleeves and get to work.

PART I

PRINCIPLES OF SELF-DISCIPLINE

∾

Success in life is commonly ascribed to a basket of personal attributes. A successful person is regarded as talented, motivated, and intelligent. They are presumed to have a positive mindset and a willingness to take strategic risks. Those who are less charitable might opine the individual is simply lucky.

While each of these elements plays a role in success, none can replace self-discipline. Talented individuals will fail if they cannot resist their impulses and devote themselves to what they must do. Likewise, motivated individuals who lack discipline typically fall short of their goals because motivation never lasts.

Nor is intelligence enough. To paraphrase Calvin

Coolidge, the world is full of intelligent people who are unrewarded with success.

And luck? It certainly plays a role, and some are indeed luckier than others. But self-discipline will always trump luck. Individuals who lack good fortune but are willing to persist when their motivation runs dry are likelier to succeed than lucky people who lack discipline. A cursory review of lottery winners reveals that sobering reality.[1]

Talent, motivation, intelligence, and luck can help you achieve your goals. But none of these are reliable. Without a rock-solid foundation of self-discipline, success will likely be sporadic, short-lived, and fleeting.

In the following pages, we'll establish what self-discipline is and what it *isn't*. You'll discover how it differs and diverges from traits that are commonly mistaken for it. We'll also dispel some of the myths and fallacies surrounding self-discipline and isolate the biggest stumbling blocks you'll likely encounter while developing it.

---

1. Hess, A. J. (2017, August 25). Here's why lottery winners go broke. *CNBC.* https://www.cnbc.com/2017/08/25/heres-why-lottery-winners-go-broke.html

SELF-DISCIPLINE DEFINED

~

" Ultimately, the only power to which man should aspire is that which he exercises over himself.

— ELIE WIESEL

S elf-discipline is universally applauded. Employers commend disciplined employees. Parents praise disciplined children. Sports enthusiasts admire disciplined athletes.

However, self-discipline is often misunderstood. Some define it too narrowly, presuming it's merely about practicing restraint. Some describe it too broadly, believing it involves everything from enduring adversity to "hustling" when you'd rather relax. Some equate it to willpower. Some think it's the same as motivation.

Self-discipline is many of these things. But none of these definitions quite hit the mark. And if we hope to master discipline, we must be able to define it in a way that resonates with us.

Over the years, I've come up with a basic definition that works well for me, and I hope it will for you, too. Here it is:

> Self-discipline is the willingness and ability to act in accordance with our goals, values, and convictions regardless of how we feel in the moment.

This is a helpful starting point. From here, we can flesh out the definition in a practical and actionable way. We can ignore vague, nebulous characterizations and focus on clear-cut aspects of self-discipline that will have a real-world impact on your life.

Self-Discipline Requires Self-Regulation

Self-discipline and self-regulation are often used interchangeably. But they are not the same thing, and it's important to distinguish between them. The latter is a facet of the former. At their simplest, they are mirror images of each other.

Self-discipline is what keeps you going when you'd rather stop. It gets you out of bed when you'd prefer to tap the snooze button on your alarm. It pushes you to clean your home when you'd rather watch television. It spurs you to do one more rep or set when you're ready to quit.

Self-regulation is what encourages you to stop when you'd rather continue. It urges you to stop playing video games when you need to study. It dissuades you from eating junk food when you're on a diet. It exhorts you to hold your tongue when angry or frustrated at someone.

Being disciplined enough to keep going when you'd rather stop requires resisting the temptation to do things that thwart your long-term goals.

Self-Discipline Requires Commitment

All of us desire specific outcomes. We want to be successful in our careers. We aspire to be physically fit. We seek financial security and might even wish to accumulate wealth. We want to learn new skills, start thriving businesses, be good parents, get more organized, and earn the respect and admiration of others.

But *having* goals isn't the same as being committed to them. Having goals is easy. Pledging to make every effort to achieve them and taking consistent action according to that pledge is difficult. It's also the difference between success and failure.

Most people fail not because of a lack of desire but because of a lack of commitment.

— VINCE LOMBARDI

Before developing and practicing self-discipline, you must commit to whatever you wish to accomplish. Your commitment will give you the strength to abstain from activities that jeopardize your goals (e.g., avoiding junk food while dieting). It'll give you the energy and motivation to press on when you feel like quitting (e.g., continuing to study when you'd rather relax in front of your television).

Your commitment is the fulcrum of your aspirations. Your self-discipline is the lever that gains purchase against the resistance you'll experience while working toward realizing them.

"Self-Discipline is Freedom"

I heard author Jocko Willink say this years ago, and I was taken aback. The claim seemed to me to be counterintuitive. After all, practicing self-discipline involves temperance and self-restraint. It demands impulse control. Self-denial is central to self-discipline, so it is *opposed* to freedom.

Or so I thought.

Further reflection led to an epiphany. Although self-discipline and freedom seemed to occupy opposing camps, they were, in fact, inseparable. Each was inextricably linked to the other. Once I recognized their relationship, I saw Willink's claim in a new light.

Satisfying your impulses may *feel* like freedom, but it's a form of self-imprisonment. You surrender control of your behaviors and decisions, and your impulses call the shots. You lose the ability and willingness to act in accordance with your goals, values, and convictions. When you constantly give in to your compulsions, you enslave yourself. You allow your urges to subjugate your conduct and ruin your resolve.

Practicing self-discipline frees you to pursue your longer-term ambitions and aspirations. Your impulses no longer control you. Instead, you have the freedom to choose and walk the path that will help you to accomplish your goals.

Everyday Examples of Self-Discipline

Now that we've defined self-discipline, let's look at a few practical examples. There's a good chance you're already disciplined in many areas of your life. That's great news because it shows you already have what it takes. Whatever you do to exert control in *one* area of your life, you can model to exert control in *others*.

But we'll get into that later. For now, here are a few examples of self-discipline in action. You're probably already practicing a few of them or did so in the past.

- Waking up early each day to get to work on time
- Studying for exams to perform well on tests
- Making cold calls to hit your lead and sales numbers
- Doing chores each week to keep your house clean
- Exercising daily to stay in shape
- Holding your tongue to avoid saying something you'll regret later (this includes social media!)
- Avoiding junk food to lose weight
- Decluttering your workstation at the end of each day to stay organized
- Saving money each month to fund a vacation
- Turning your phone off while you work to avoid distractions
- Staying in touch with friends to maintain those relationships
- Addressing personal hygiene to stay healthy and look presentable
- Being on time to show respect to others
- Meditating to lower your stress and improve your focus
- Meeting deadlines to bolster your career
- Keeping your promises to show that you're dependable
- Developing new habits to improve your quality of life
- Taking regular breaks to stay fresh and creative

- Reading self-improvement books to increase your knowledge and adjust your mindset

You're undoubtedly practicing self-discipline, even if your actions have become so routine that you don't realize it. It's important to recognize this fact because it'll fuel your motivation to become disciplined in every aspect of your life you desire. It demonstrates that self-discipline isn't unachievable. On the contrary, you've already achieved it! Now, it's a matter of developing and applying it elsewhere.

WHY SELF-DISCIPLINE IS IMPORTANT

~

66 Self-control is the chief element in self-respect,
and self-respect is the chief element in
courage.

— THUCYDIDES

I n the previous section, we broached the idea that
discipline is freedom. We discussed how controlling
your impulses and practicing temperance can help
you to achieve your aspirations. Doing so allows you to
conduct yourself according to your values and convictions
while accomplishing anything you set out to do.

But that was the bird's-eye view. Here, we'll delve

deeper into the details. I'll show you how practicing discipline will positively affect important areas of your life.

It's one thing to recognize that self-control is beneficial. Again, nearly everyone accepts this fact. But it's also important to realize that developing and maintaining it requires time and effort. So it's worth taking a moment to appreciate why you should make the investment.

Habit Development & Habit Interruption

It isn't easy to create new habits. Doing so usually involves acting in a way that contradicts your everyday behaviors and routines. It matters not whether the practices in question are familiar or unfamiliar. It takes work to incorporate them into your regimen and stick to them over the long haul. It conflicts with deeply ingrained patterns.

It's similarly challenging to break old habits. Practicing familiar routines releases dopamine in your brain. Dopamine is a potent neurotransmitter that induces feelings of pleasure and satisfaction. Understandably, you crave such releases over and over. This is the engine that drives compulsive behaviors. It's also the reason interrupting these behaviors is so tough.

Self-discipline is pivotal to forming new habits and ceasing old ones. It empowers you to act consistently undeterred by familiar urges and impulses.

Taking Action

Accomplishing anything requires action. No goal can be realized without doing something purposeful toward its achievement. This is the reason that procrastination is so problematic. It involves *inaction*, the most effortless practice to perform. Putting off doing something requires zero effort.

You might fail to take action for countless reasons, many of which have nothing to do with laziness. But regardless of the reason, the antidote is the same: self-discipline. Discipline will help you to follow through on your plans, intentions, and promising ideas when you feel compelled to put them off (or abandon them altogether).

Goal Achievement

During childhood, authority figures compel you to act. Your parents encourage you to study, eat well, and get sufficient sleep. Your teachers push you to read certain books and master specific curricula. Your coaches drive you to perform select drills related to your chosen sport.

This "pressure" continues in some respects during adulthood. For example, your boss urges you to complete tasks related to your job. Law enforcement officers require you to conform to local laws and ordinances.

But no such external pressure exists when it comes to achieving personal goals. No one is going to force you to follow through on your aspirations. You'll have to rely on yourself to accomplish something (e.g., get into shape, learn a second language, write a novel, etc.).

This means being disciplined enough to resist present bias. Present bias prioritizes present rewards over future rewards (e.g., eating a donut rather than sticking to a healthy diet). It always conflicts with goal achievement; it goads you to postpone your goals in favor of immediate gratification.

Self-discipline is necessary to oppose it.

Confidence and Poise

Confidence and poise largely stem from personal achievement. When you accomplish something important to you, you feel empowered. You feel you can control outcomes, particularly as they relate to your desires. Here are a few examples:

- Completing your daily to-do list
- Asking someone you like out on a date
- Learning to play a new song on your guitar
- Losing a specific amount of weight
- Achieving a perfect score on a test

Accomplishing these things builds your confidence and improves your presence of mind during times of stress. It gives you pride in your ability to follow through and self-assurance that you can remain calm, composed, and effective when necessary.

But before this occurs, you must possess the self-discipline needed to see things through to completion in the first place.

Relationships

Your relationships thrive or deteriorate based on your decisions and behaviors. Treating others respectfully, communicating empathetically, and showing compassion strengthen your bonds with them. Conversely, breaking their trust, communicating poorly, and showing indifference or callousness weaken the bonds and ruin the intimacy you share with them.

Self-discipline plays a pivotal role in cultivating and nurturing successful relationships. It prevents you from acting impulsively in ways that offend or hurt others (e.g., cheating on your spouse). It helps you regulate your emotions and avoid lashing out when others disappoint you (e.g., responding angrily when a friend cancels plans at the last minute). Self-discipline allows you to remain calm and resolve conflicts productively and healthily (e.g., de-escalating tension between you and an agitated coworker).

Self-discipline engenders harmony, while impulsiveness often leads to strife.

Career Growth

Office politics aside, your career trajectory stems from your skills, decisions, conduct, and resilience. Perform well in these areas, and your career will improve, and your prospects for future success will increase. Perform poorly, and your career will languish, and your prospects will contract.

Your long-term performance will stem largely from the degree of self-discipline you practice. Your discipline will help you to make sound decisions, work productively, and meet deadlines. As mentioned above, it'll allow you to work harmoniously with difficult coworkers, including your bosses. Your discipline will help you to concentrate, ignoring distractions around you. It'll encourage you to deliver high-quality work when your impulsive self would rather cut corners.

Can you have a successful career without self-discipline? Perhaps. But the odds are against you. When you develop self-discipline, you stack the odds in your favor.

Resilience

Life is challenging. While thoughtful planning and good decisions can help you avoid *some* of life's struggles, you can't avoid them all. You can't *plan* for them all. As the Stoics of old knew, you can only control your response to failure, adversity, and setbacks.

Resilience is your ability to bounce back when things go wrong. It's an inner strength that helps you endure the stress and pressure life imposes on you. It's a foundational toughness that pushes you to hold the line and persist when you'd rather surrender. It encourages you to excel regardless of your limitations.

Self-discipline is a prerequisite of resilience. To become resilient, you must resist your impulses, manage your emotions, and uphold your boundaries. Only then will you be truly ready to face and overcome life's challenges.

Spillover Effect

This is a phenomenon typically referenced in the context of economics. It refers to events that occur in one region due to events in another. For example, when the U.S. imposed tariffs on China in 2008, it set in motion a trade war that impacted U.S. imports from other countries.

This phenomenon also occurs when you cultivate self-discipline. As you develop self-control, you'll notice it "spills over" into other areas of your life. For example, sticking to a healthy diet will inspire you to learn to cook. Sticking to a daily workout regimen will encourage you to avoid junk food. Becoming less impulsive will enhance your relationships, improve your finances, and boost your self-confidence.

Self-Discipline is Your Secret Weapon

While it's universally applauded, few people possess self-discipline. Few put in the time and do the hard work to develop it. You don't need me to convince you. The evidence is on display everywhere.

Motorists regularly react in rage over perceived slights. Spouses commonly scream at each other and their children in public. Students neglect to study for exams. Employees gossip about each other. Meanwhile, obesity rates continue to climb in developed countries.

Self-discipline gives you an advantage. It allows you to avoid the petty nonsense that embroils others. It gives you the ability to de-escalate situations with an air of calmness. It helps you focus on what you need and want to do rather than get sidetracked by endless distractions.

Self-discipline is your secret weapon in achieving success in every area of your life. But to cultivate it, you must be willing to delay gratification.

SELF-DISCIPLINE AND DELAYED GRATIFICATION

~

" The ability to subordinate an impulse to a value is the essence of the proactive person.

— STEPHEN R. COVEY

Given the option, we prefer to enjoy a reward now rather than in the future. We're also willing to discount the value of the reward based on when we receive it. Economists refer to this as time preference. Those with a high time preference are willing to apply a greater discount to enjoy immediate satisfaction.

For example, suppose someone offers to give you $100 in 30 days. You also have the option to receive a lesser amount immediately. If you have a high time preference, you might accept a deeply discounted $5 today. If you have a low time preference, you may be willing to take no less than $75 today. Otherwise, you prefer to receive the total amount in 30 days.

A low time preference means you're willing to delay gratification so that you can enjoy greater rewards in the future. This is a core tenet of self-discipline. Sadly, it doesn't come easily for most of us. We tend to be impatient when it comes to pleasure of any sort.

But if we train ourselves to *wait*, we stand to benefit in ways that make our restraint worthwhile. We allow ourselves to act with greater purpose toward achieving our longer-term goals and aspirations.

Delayed Gratification 101

Delaying gratification means resisting the temptations of the present with the expectation that doing so will help you get something you truly want in the future. This willingness to forgo immediate satisfaction always comes at a cost: You must do without something *now* to receive something better *later*.

Sometimes, the future reward will bring you greater happiness or fulfillment. For example, eating junk food in the present is tempting, but staying fit will improve your sleep, relieve stress, and boost your mood. If you're an athlete, skipping workouts is tempting, but continuing to show up will help you to perform better later.

Sometimes, the future reward is the avoidance of something unpleasant. For example, you may be tempted or pressured to try an illicit substance. Practicing temperance allows you to avoid addiction. You may be tempted to fool around with a coworker showering you with flirtatious attention. Refraining from doing so will allow you to avoid professional consequences in the event of a breakup (e.g., office gossip, harassment, termination, etc.).

Delaying gratification is always practiced with a goal in mind. Here, clarity and specificity matter. The more precise your goal, the easier you'll be able to resist temptations.

The Stanford Marshmallow Test

The famous 1972 Stanford marshmallow test[1] provided insight into children's ability to delay rewards and associated this ability with later success. Dozens of children were given a marshmallow and a choice: they could eat it immediately or resist the temptation for 15 minutes and be rewarded with a second marshmallow.

The researchers found that when the children were distracted from thinking about the reward, they were more inclined to wait. Conversely, the more the children thought about the reward, the less willing they were to wait. The researchers checked in with the study participants over the following 40 years. They discovered that the early ability to delay gratification was associated with numerous success markers later (better academic performance, greater ability to cope with stress, etc.).[2]

These were valuable insights. However, it wasn't until follow-up studies were conducted that researchers learned why many children had difficulty delaying gratification. Thinking about the reward was only one factor, arguably not the most impactful one.

Why Delaying Gratification is Difficult

It came down to a matter of trust.

In 2012, researchers at the University of Rochester conducted a follow-up marshmallow test.[3] They wanted to understand how great a role uncertainty played a role in children's willingness to delay rewards.

The researchers divided 28 children into two groups. A promise was made to both groups before the children received marshmallows. The researchers broke their promise to the first group and made good on it for the second group. Marshmallows were then distributed to the children, who were given the same option as in the 1972 Stanford study: eat the marshmallows immediately or wait and receive another.

The researchers found that the children in the first group waited a mean duration of three minutes and two seconds before eating their marshmallows. The children in the second group waited four times as long (12 minutes and two seconds). The researchers surmised that the first group was less willing to wait because they didn't trust that they would receive a second marshmallow. The precursory broken promise made them doubtful they would be rewarded for their temperance.

This test provided much greater insight into why people find it difficult to delay gratification. When you're uncertain whether practicing self-control in the present will yield the attendant rewards in the future, you're less likely to resist temptations and deny yourself.

For example, let's suppose you'd like to get into shape. You're more likely to eat junk food in the present if you're doubtful that you'll follow through on this goal. Or let's say you need to study for an exam. You're more likely to abandon studying and attend a get-together with friends if you doubt studying will affect your grade.

Uncertainty is the biggest reason it's challenging to practice impulse control. The good news is that it reveals how you can get better at it.

3 Quick Tips to Get Better at Delaying Gratification

The ability to delay gratification is like a muscle. The more you use it, the stronger it gets. Here are three ways to give this muscle the workout it needs. Do these regularly, and you'll find it increasingly easier to maintain control.

1. Start by resisting small temptations

You'd do crunches to strengthen your core (pelvis, stomach, etc.). But you wouldn't start with ten sets of 50 crunches per day. You'd start smaller — e.g., three sets of ten crunches — and build up as your core strengthens.

Approach delaying gratification in the same way. Work on resisting small temptations in the beginning. Scale up as your ability grows.

For example, let's say you're addicted to sugar. Rather than avoiding sugar for the next six months, commit to avoiding sugar for the next 24 hours. Once you're able to do this successfully, move the goalposts. Commit to avoiding sugar for the next 72 hours. Keep pushing the goalposts as your delaying gratification "muscle" strengthens.

2. Recognize the cost of a temptation

Every temptation comes at a cost. It's natural to overlook this cost because the promise of immediate pleasure obfuscates it. This is especially true of costs imposed far in the future. The further away it is, the harder it is to exert impulse control in the present.

For example, let's say you regularly snack on junk food. The cost to your health is not immediate. It's something you'll pay for in the future. This fact makes it difficult to resist the appeal of your favorite treats. You're instead focused on the pleasure you'll experience in the moment.

Remind yourself about the cost attached to the temptation you're struggling with. In our example, this might include diabetes, heart disease, hypertension, and obesity. When you think about the price you'll pay for satisfying an immediate craving, you'll be more disposed to resist the urge.

3. Attach targets to goals

Recall the 2012 study that revealed that children doubtful about receiving future rewards for their current temperance were less likely to wait. Trust played a significant role. The more uncertain they were about the future (i.e., receiving a second marshmallow), the less likely they were to show restraint (i.e., resisting the urge to eat the first marshmallow).

This response isn't limited to children. Adults are the same way when deciding whether to satisfy or resist cravings. For example, if you're convinced the economy is going to crash, you'll be less inclined to save money, preferring instead to spend it. If you feel that you'll never be able to get into shape, you'll be more willing to eat the sugary treat you crave.

Here's how to short-circuit this response: attach targets to every goal.

For example, don't just "save money." Instead, commit to saving "$5,000 by July 1st." The amount and date give you something specific to aim for. Don't just aspire to "get in shape." Instead, commit to "losing 15 lb and achieving a 20% body fat percentage by July 1st." Again, these provide specific targets to shoot for.

The next time you're craving something that conflicts with one of your goals, you'll find it easier to resist the temptation. These targets give you something definitive to focus on.

Delaying gratification is one facet of practicing self-discipline, albeit an important one. How you manage stress is another…

---

1. Mischel, W., & Ebbesen, E. B. (1970). Attention in delay of gratification. *Journal of Personality and Social Psychology, 16*(2), 329–337.
2. Mischel, W., Shoda, Y., & Rodriguez, M. (1989b). Delay of gratification in children. *Science, 244*(4907), 933–938.
3. Kidd, C., Palmeri, H., & Aslin, R. N. (2013). Rational snacking: Young children's decision-making on the marshmallow task is moderated by beliefs about environmental reliability. *Cognition, 126*(1), 109–114.

SELF-DISCIPLINE DURING TIMES OF STRESS

∾

66 Self-discipline is a form of freedom. Freedom from laziness and lethargy, freedom from expectations and demands of others, freedom from weakness and fear -- and doubt.

— HARVEY A. DORFMAN

S tress and self-discipline share an antagonistic relationship. They work toward conflicting ends. They are constantly butting heads. The more ground you give to one of them, the less ground the other can hold.

There are many causes of stress. But one of the most

common and influential is a feeling of lack of control. When you feel like you can't control what's happening around you, you experience stress. The greater the anticipated impact of those circumstances on your life, the more stress you feel. Ironically, the more stress you experience, the less control you think you can exert.

It's a terrible, debilitating cycle.

Below, we'll take a closer look at the relationship between stress and self-discipline. I'll show you how each affects the other and give you some quick tips on staying in control whenever stress rears its ugly head.

How Stress Impacts Your Self-Control

If you've ever consumed too much wine, you know first-hand its effect on your self-discipline. Your impulse control erodes, and the boundaries you've set to help manage your emotions crumble. In this state, delaying gratification seems ridiculous.

Stress has a similar effect. Under extreme pressure, the amygdala — the area of your brain that manages your survival instincts — kicks into gear. It notes the source of the stress (environmental or biological) and tries to determine its potential impact. You've heard of the brain's fight-or-flight response. The amygdala is in charge of that response.

Before the amygdala compels you to do something you regret, it checks in with the prefrontal cortex. This part of your brain manages your emotions (it does many things, but let's focus on emotions here). The amygdala tells the prefrontal cortex, "We've got a serious problem." The prefrontal cortex responds to the amygdala, "Calm down. We can handle this rationally." Then, it decides how to respond to the stressor.

Ideally, this process would be enough. But humans are sensitive to high stress levels (yes, even those individuals who claim to "eat stress for breakfast"). It still grinds down our impulse control.

For example, recall the last time a motorist cut you off, causing you to swerve suddenly in your lane. This stress-inducing event activated your amygdala, which told your prefrontal cortex, "Red alert! We need to respond to this knucklehead!" The prefrontal cortex countered with, "Wait a second. Calm down. We're safe. Disaster has been averted." Yet, you still felt compelled to express your disapproval to the offending motorist, perhaps using a particular finger. (No judgment. I've done the same thing.)

Despite your internal stress-response systems working constantly to keep you safe, you still lost emotional control. You experienced a temporary loss of *impulse* control, which might have ironically put you in harm's way (road rage is a thing).

Stress can wreak havoc on your emotional self-regulation and, thereby, your ability to practice self-discipline. Let's now take a look at the other side of this relationship.

How Self-Discipline Keeps Stress at Bay

As much as stress can sap your self-discipline, practicing self-discipline can help you to feel less stressed. The reason harkens back to one of the leading causes of stress: feeling that you lack control and being incensed by this circumstance.

Two factors play important roles related to this issue. First, when disciplined, you're more inclined to avoid situations that lead to unnecessary stress.

For example, saving money each month provides a financial cushion; you're less likely to experience stress related to living paycheck to paycheck. Studying prepares you for exams; you're less likely to feel stressed about your grades. Taking your vehicle in for regular maintenance prevents it from breaking down; you're less likely to experience the anxiety of being stranded by the side of the road.

Self-discipline helps you to make better decisions. While stress is an avoidable part of life, these better decisions will help you to steer clear of *needless* stress.

The second factor is that practicing self-discipline helps you manage your response to stressors outside your influence.

For example, you can't control traffic congestion on your way home from the office; recognizing this fact helps you accept it rather than fuming. You can't control the weather; acknowledging this allows you to respond rationally to it (e.g., putting snow chains on your vehicle) instead of obsessing about it. You can't control others' behaviors;

conceding this helps you to stay calm and manage your emotions instead of feeling offended and outraged when others behave poorly.

This second factor touches on a core principle of stoicism. Rather than allowing yourself to feel stressed about circumstances you cannot control, focus on how you respond to those circumstances.

 You have power over your mind — not outside events. Realize this, and you will find strength.

— MARCUS AURELIUS

How to Stay in Control During Stressful Times

Stoicism is a distant cousin to self-discipline, sharing traits while remaining distinct from one another. While practicing stoicism is usually helpful for staying in control, that advice is too broad. So, let's cover a few specific tips that you can use *today* to stay disciplined when life gets stressful.

The first step is to figure out the cause of the stress. Are you under pressure to meet a strict deadline (time stress)? Are you fighting with a friend or loved one (relational stress)? Are you struggling to make ends meet (financial stress)? Are you suffering from a debilitating illness (physiological stress)? Are you feeling depressed (emotional stress)? Once you've identified the reason, you can take purposeful action to resolve or counter it.

Second, think about how you'll feel — and the consequences you'll suffer — if you surrender control. For example, suppose you're on a diet, but work-related stress makes you susceptible to junk food cravings. Consider the guilt and shame you'll experience if you abandon your diet during this stressful time. Or suppose you're having a disagreement with your spouse. Imagine the repercussions of acting on your impulses and saying something spiteful. Thinking about how you'll feel *afterward* will help you to resist behaving recklessly or with shortsightedness.

Third, remind yourself that *you* are responsible for your actions and decisions. Your circumstances may not be your fault, but how you respond to them is your responsibility. For example, suppose your spouse says unkind things to you during a disagreement. That's not your fault. But you *are* accountable for what you say in return. Acknowledging your agency is powerful. It's a glorious reminder that *you* can decide whether you remain disciplined, regardless of what life throws at you.

Most people can tolerate an absurd amount of stress — certainly more than they imagine. In most cases, their biggest stumbling block is their mindset. If you practice the three tactics above whenever stress rears, you'll find it much easier to stay in control and resist temptations.

In the next section, we'll clarify and debunk several common misunderstandings and illusions about self-discipline.

COMMON MISCONCEPTIONS ABOUT
SELF-DISCIPLINE

66 Self-discipline is the ability to make yourself do
what you should do when you should do it,
whether you feel like it or not.

— ELBERT HUBBARD

Many people perceive self-discipline in ways
that discourage them from pursuing it. They
have false ideas about what discipline is (and
isn't), how to develop it, and what it means to practice it
daily. Sadly, these ideas cause many folks to avoid building
discipline despite recognizing its importance to their long-
term success.

Below, we'll investigate the seven most common fallacies about self-discipline. If you've been avoiding improving this area of your life, you may have done so because of one or more of them. So, let's hold these seven fallacies up to the light and check whether they hold water (spoiler: they don't).

Fallacy #1: Self-discipline is identical to willpower

People use these terms interchangeably. But there's a critical difference between them, and this difference defines one of the fundamental principles of discipline.

Self-discipline embodies an organized, carefully thought-out approach to life that aligns with your values, convictions, and long-term goals. It involves habits and routines that support your ambition to be the person you want to be.

Willpower is the self-control you exert to resist your immediate impulses. You can delay gratification in the present.

For example, let's say that you want to get into shape. To do so, you decide to work out each day at your local gym. Self-discipline would involve habits that support this goal, such as getting up at 6:00 a.m. each morning. Getting up at this time would become a part of your routine. It would become automatic. Willpower would involve resisting the urge to hit snooze when your alarm goes off tomorrow morning.

Both self-discipline and willpower play decisive roles in

goal achievement. But they are not the same. They are entirely distinct from one another, and it's important to note that distinction. (We'll examine willpower in greater detail in the next chapter.)

Fallacy #2: Self-discipline requires being emotionless

The familiar image of a self-disciplined person is practically a cliche. This mythic individual is dispassionate, possesses an iron will, and does… not… falter. EVER. They are a machine for whom defeat is inconceivable. This fabled hero is emotionless, personifying pledges like "failure is not an option."

This person is a work of fiction. They don't exist.

The reality is that building and maintaining self-discipline requires emotional awareness. It demands that you know where your mind is at all times. If you want to exert impulse control immediately and over the long run, you must understand why you feel compelled to behave in specific ways. Only by recognizing your compulsions and determining whether they're genuinely attuned to your needs will you be able to resist them calmly.

Fallacy #3: Self-discipline is not for everyone

No one is born with self-discipline. It does not come naturally to some but is intrinsically difficult for others. It's not genetic.

The biggest problem with this misconception is that it

causes people to believe that building their discipline is futile. Or at least, it's too difficult and not worth investing their time and effort.

Let's set the record straight.

Everyone starts from the same jumping-off point (birth). From that point, self-discipline is learned, practiced, and honed over time. Although some folks receive more help than others early in their lives (e.g., parental encouragement), anyone can cultivate it. With commitment and consistent practice, the playing field levels out.

Fallacy #4: Self-discipline limits your freedom

It may seem as though self-discipline is the antithesis of freedom. The freedom to eat what you want. The freedom to say what you want. The freedom to do whatever you want to do whenever you want to do it. This viewpoint understandably turns off many people from the idea of cultivating self-discipline. After all, why would anyone want to restrict their life willingly?

But this is a common error. The reality is considerably different and usually requires a significant shift in perspective.

Self-discipline doesn't limit your freedom. It *gives* you freedom. The freedom to pursue the goals you want to achieve. The freedom to live the life you want to live. The freedom to be the person you truly want to be. Self-discipline gives you independence from your current urges and emotions, freeing you to make choices consistent with your values, convictions, and ambitions.

Fallacy #5: Self-discipline gives you control

We want to feel as though we're in control. This universal desire stems from a severe dislike — and even fear — of uncertainty. It's also a pipe dream, and building self-discipline will not (*cannot*) change this fact.

You don't control other people; you have no authority over their motives, actions, and reactions. You don't control your circumstances; you have no jurisdiction over natural events, market gyrations, and civil disturbances.

The only thing you control is yourself. You're in charge of your behavior. You're in charge of your actions and reactions. You're in charge of your thoughts, beliefs, and emotions. You're in charge of your values and goals and whether you allow yourself to be swayed by temptations.

This is more powerful than it seems. Self-discipline leads to self-mastery, which gives you the autonomy to evaluate situations, weigh your options, make reasoned decisions, and take purposeful action.

Fallacy #6: Self-discipline is just saying "no"

Self-discipline is often oversimplified. It's commonly generalized to saying "no" to your impulses and compulsions. "No" to the urge to eat ice cream while on a diet. "No" to the temptation of pursuing an attractive coworker when you're married. "No" to the itch of responding in anger when someone treats you disrespectfully.

The willingness to say "no" defines self-*control*, not self-discipline. The former is merely one facet of the latter. It's critical, but the latter encompasses much more than this single trait.

When you say "no" to temptations, you do so in the moment. You're presented with an impulse or urge, and you decide then and there to resist it. Self-discipline stems from a longer-term viewpoint. It arises from goals, which influence your decisions and actions over a prolonged period (even a lifetime!).

Saying "no" to eating a bowl of ice cream after dinner tonight exemplifies self-control. Refraining from eating ice cream entirely because you want to stay in shape is an example of self-discipline.

Fallacy #7: Maintaining self-discipline is difficult

This is arguably the biggest hindrance for people who aspire to build self-discipline. They assume the experience will be difficult and unpleasant. So, they give up before they truly get started.

There are two points to address here.

First, living life in the absence of self-discipline seems easy, but that's an illusion. It is perpetuated by making decisions while viewing life through a snapshot of the present. Giving in to your urges and impulses right now is almost sure to carry consequences in the future. For example, eating ice cream after dinner is easy (giving in to temptations is always easy). But if you do it every night, you'll eventually experience weight gain, digestive problems, and other health issues.

Second, maintaining self-discipline is only tricky when it's unsupported by habits and routines. With the proper habits and routines in place, maintaining it becomes much more manageable. For example, suppose you usually get out of bed at 8:00 a.m. You'll probably find it difficult to wake up at 5:00 a.m. tomorrow. But if you've risen at 5:00 a.m. each morning over the last several weeks, waking up at that time tomorrow will be second nature to you.

Is self-discipline challenging to develop and maintain? Yes, but only in a minimal context. The right approach makes it far less challenging, and your success is guaranteed. (In *Part II*, I'll take you through this approach step by step.)

I promised earlier that we'd take a deeper dive into willpower related to self-discipline. It's time for me to make good on that promise.

SELF-DISCIPLINE VS. WILLPOWER

~

    You will never have a greater or lesser dominion than that over yourself… the height of a man's success is gauged by his self-mastery; the depth of his failure by his self-abandonment… and this is the law of eternal justice.

— LEONARDO DA VINCI

We noted in the preceding chapter that self-discipline and willpower are distinct. So, we won't rehash that topic here. A simple way to remember how they differ is to think of self-discipline as a way of life and willpower as the choices you make in the moment.

This doesn't mean that willpower is unimportant, however. It's vital to building self-discipline, especially in the early stages. It's *necessary*. With that in mind, I'll explain how it works, highlight its most significant limitation, and give you a few actionable tips for strengthening it.

How Willpower Works

Willpower is more complicated than it seems. You use it every day to make choices. But behind each choice, a battle is waged in your brain.

Your prefrontal cortex kicks into gear whenever you're about to choose between multiple options. It sits in the front region of your brain and regulates a host of executive functions, including decision-making and self-regulation.

This area of the brain isn't the stalwart paragon of discipline we imagine (or hope) it to be. It's susceptible to temptation. It recognizes the rewards and consequences, both short-term and long-term, presented by every option and sometimes becomes conflicted. For example, when you see your favorite candy bar, your prefrontal cortex weighs how tasty it is against the fact that it's unhealthy. You want to eat it, but you also want to be healthy. This conundrum causes cognitive dissonance.

At this point in the decision-making process, your willpower comes into play. If you have strong willpower, you'll resist the urge to eat the candy bar. If you lack willpower, that candy bar is destined for your tummy.

This process seems simple, but it requires a lot of energy. Faced with conflicting choices throughout the day, your prefrontal cortex slowly becomes fatigued. As your day progresses, it becomes increasingly difficult to resist temptations. By the end of the day, you're mentally and emotionally depleted, and it's much harder to resist eating that candy bar.

This introduces the paramount limitation of willpower.

The Problem With Willpower

You can already see the problem. Willpower is like the fuel stored in your vehicle's gas tank. The volume of fuel in the tank depletes as you use it. The more you use, the less you're left with. Your tank eventually runs dry — at least, until you can refill it by getting a good night's rest.

You might assume you can conserve this "fuel" until you truly need it. But multiple factors conspire against you. Recall the last time you visited your local grocery store or shopping mall. Do you remember the hundreds of items shrewdly positioned to get your attention? These items forced you to make a mountain of micro-decisions, and each one whittled away your willpower.

Your immediate surroundings aren't the only factor working against you. The quality of your sleep also plays a role. In a study published in 2014, researchers described results that suggested that even a single night of poor sleep impaired the function of the prefrontal cortex.[1]

These are the main issues with willpower. They are the reason you can't rely on willpower alone to resist your impulses and make good choices.

Why Self-Discipline Always Trumps Willpower in the Long Run

Because willpower is a depleting resource, you face an ever-present risk of not having enough when needed. Moreover, factors outside your control heavily influence the amount at your disposal.

If you have a particularly exhausting day, you'll have nothing left in the "tank." If you sleep poorly, you'll start with far less than had you slept well. Either way, you'll find it more difficult to resist temptations, control your urges, and regulate your emotions.

This is the reason self-discipline upstages willpower. When you rely on self-discipline, you're depending on habits. Once they're developed, these habits spur behaviors via a neurological loop. Cues trigger them as part of a routine, which ends with rewards that satisfy cravings and provide reinforcement.

Your habits are not a depletable resource. You can rely on them from the moment you wake up in the morning until you go to bed in the evening. You never have to worry about whether you have enough in the tank.

3 Quick Tips For Increasing Your Willpower

Although willpower suffers from a serious shortcoming (its depletable nature), it is pivotal for delaying gratification in the present. This is especially true when you haven't yet developed habits to do the heavy lifting for you.

In short, more willpower is better than less. But you won't need it as much once you establish good habits that support your long-term self-discipline. But for now, let's strengthen this muscle so you can use it as a short-term tool. Here are three quick tips.

First, use temptation bundling.[2] It's a strategy that uses instant gratification to spur you to do things that require willpower. For example, let's say you want to listen to your favorite podcast. It's a guilty pleasure. You also need to walk your dog. With temptation bundling, you'd allow yourself to listen to the podcast, but only while walking your dog.

Second, track your decisions and behaviors. Look for cues that precede poor ones, and try to minimize those cues. For example, you might discover that you're most tempted to eat junk food when stressed out. Rather than trying to avoid junk food through sheer force of will, try to resolve the most prevalent stressors in your life.

Third, improve your sleep quality. (I know, it's easier said than done, but hear me out.) Here are a few ideas:

- Create a sleep schedule, and stick to it. Go to bed at the same time each evening. Get out of bed at the same time each morning.

- Avoid alcohol, caffeine, and large meals several hours before bed.
- Don't use your phone or other devices in bed.
- Don't watch television in bed.
- Take a warm shower a couple of hours before bedtime.
- Avoid using too many blankets (a high body temperature disrupts sleep).
- Keep your bedroom semi-dark at night.

Sleep quality is a vast subject that deserves its own book. But the simple tips have improved my sleep, and I'd be willing to bet they'll improve yours, too.

We now understand how willpower works, how it compares to self-discipline, and how to increase it while forming good habits. Let's turn our attention to motivation.

––––––––––––––––––––––

1. Vartanian, O., Bouak, F., Caldwell, J. L., Cheung, B., Cupchik, G. C., Jobidon, M., Lam, Q., Nakashima, A., Paul, M., Peng, H., Silvia, P. J., & Smith, I. (2014). The effects of a single night of sleep deprivation on fluency and prefrontal cortex function during divergent thinking. *Frontiers in Human Neuroscience, 8.*

2. The term was coined by Wharton professor Katherine Milkman. Along with two other researchers, she authored a fascinating study of temptation bundling:

    Milkman, K. L., Minson, J. A., & Volpp, K. G. (2014). Holding the Hunger Games hostage at the Gym: An evaluation of temptation bundling. *Management Science, 60*(2), 283–299.

SELF-DISCIPLINE VS. MOTIVATION

66 Don't expect to be motivated every day to get out there and make things happen. You won't be. Don't count on motivation, count on discipline.

—JOCKO WILLINK

Motivation is the instigator behind your actions. It encourages you to do what's necessary to achieve goals that are important to you. It drives you to make things happen when you're dissatisfied with your circumstances. It pushes you to take action when stasis becomes uncomfortable or untenable.

Motivation is important, and I'll show you how to use it well below. But it's equally important to realize that it's overrated. Like willpower, it's beset with limitations that make it unreliable. Moreover, it has a dark side that's rarely discussed but vital to recognize.

How Motivation Works

Motivation springs from many sources. Some are intrinsic, while others are extrinsic (more on this in a moment), and they often change as you age.

Your parents likely influenced your behaviors and decisions during childhood. Consequences were attached to poor behavior, and rewards were linked to good behavior. Your teachers probably exerted a similar influence. Along the way, you modified your behavior to align with their expectations.

As you grew older, your parents and teachers had less influence on you. You reached adulthood, and they became less authoritative in your eyes. Your parents could no longer ground you for poor behavior (or increase your weekly allowance for good behavior). Your teachers could no longer threaten you with failing grades. The sources of your motivation shifted to your friends, significant others, and employers. You adapted your behaviors, in part, to please them and meet *their* expectations.

These influences are examples of *extrinsic* motivation. They promise (or imply) rewards and consequences that are external to you. The more you value these rewards and dread these consequences, the more effective they are as motivators for you.

Intrinsic motivation stems from within. Your behaviors and decisions are motivated by internal rewards and consequences. Your beliefs, values, likes and dislikes, and goals and aspirations inform these. They are attached to your identity.

For example, you tend to your garden because you enjoy gardening. You help a friend move because doing so makes you feel good. You refrain from eating junk food because you want to feel better. Your actions are not motivated by pressure from others, but rather your sense of self that defines who you are.

You'll encounter both types of motivation throughout your life. But because intrinsic motivators are attached to your identity, they're arguably more powerful than extrinsic ones. You feel their influence more intensely. For example, if integrity is one of your core values, you'll be motivated to act honorably no matter your circumstances. Meanwhile, extrinsic motivators such as receiving airline miles for using a specific credit card have less persistent influence on you.

To be clear, both types of motivation are beneficial. You can use both to prompt yourself to take action. You can employ both to build and strengthen your self-discipline. But it's important to note how they differ from one another to appreciate how they affect your actions and decisions.

Motivation vs. Willpower

For the sake of clarity and precision, let's contrast motivation and willpower. We must use these terms correctly to understand their effects on our self-discipline.

We noted earlier that willpower is your ability to resist your immediate impulses. It's your capacity for delaying gratification in the present. This includes everything from avoiding the candy bar calling your name while on a diet to journaling when you'd rather watch television.

Motivation is the *reason* you want to do something. For example, *why* are you on a diet? To feel better? To look better? To build your confidence? Why are you journaling? To reduce your stress? To record your thoughts for later review? To cope with negative emotions and improve your mental health?

Both willpower and motivation are essential. Both influence your decisions and actions in the present, informed by the goals you want to achieve. To that end, both are potent allies in the fight to develop self-discipline. But neither is reliable.

Earlier, we likened willpower to the fuel in a tank that depletes as you use it and eventually runs dry. Similarly, it's impossible to feel motivated consistently over the long run. Your motivation ebbs and flows with your emotions, energy, and the impact of your immediate circumstances on your comfort. In short, sometimes you're just not "feeling it."

Worse, motivation has a dark side.

The Dark Side of Motivation

We tend to see motivation in a positive light. We get excited and inspired to do something and take intentional action, driven by optimism and confidence. We feel energized to "chase our dreams" and "follow our passion." We feel galvanized to "go after what we want."

But this cheery outlook hides a darker side to motivation. If we ignore or overlook it, we risk surrendering our headspace to negative emotions. Motivation can spring from fear, rage, jealousy, and disgust as quickly as it can from inspiration, excitement, optimism, and confidence.

The problem is that negative emotions do more harm than good when building and maintaining self-discipline.[1] They prevent you from reasoning. They encourage you to behave in troublesome and reckless ways, driven by a cynical urgency that may have nothing to do with your long-term goals and aspirations.

For example, let's say you fear losing your job. This fear might spur you to do things antithetical to your long-term career goals. Or suppose you look in the mirror and are revolted by what you see. This revulsion can lead to self-loathing, which spurs you to go on an unhealthy crash diet rather than adopting healthy habits that help you to get into shape.

Negative emotions *can* motivate you to control your impulses and delay gratification, two critical fundamentals of self-discipline. But they do so in an untenable way. Emotions like fear, disgust, anger, and shame can harm your mental (and physical) health. If they're allowed to persist unchecked, they'll crush your optimism and fuel a lasting cynicism that counters — and slowly ruins — your aspirations.

The Achilles Heel of Motivation

Like willpower, motivation has a central weak point. This failing is its Achilles heel, and it makes it unreliable.

The main problem with motivation is that it happens entirely in your mind. Consequently, it's susceptible to your mental state at any given moment, a state that's heavily influenced by numerous factors. Here are a few of them:

- Stress
- Fear
- Anger
- Emotional exhaustion
- Mental trauma
- Self-doubt
- Self-criticism
- Imposter syndrome
- Boredom
- Burnout
- Lack of sleep
- Hunger
- Feeling overwhelmed

These factors are toxic to your motivation. They sabotage it and prevent you from acting upon it. They are why you can feel inspired to accomplish something yet fail to follow through.

For example, how many people do you know who are motivated to save money but continue to live paycheck to paycheck? How many people do you know who profess to want to get into shape but continue to sleep in rather than work out? How many do you know who aspire to be promoted at their jobs but continue to do the absolute minimum?

That's why motivation in and of itself is useless. It makes you feel inspired and excited to act, but these feelings amount to nothing if you neglect to follow through. On the other hand, if you know how to *draw* on your motivation to spur you to take immediate, purposeful action, it can be a powerful tool in your self-discipline tool chest.

Put plainly, motivation is a flawed but potent stimulant. It's fleeting, unreliable, and short-lived, but it's beneficial when appropriately harnessed.

3 Quick Tips For Using Motivation To Spur Action

Even though motivation is a fickle friend, you can take steps to induce it and use it to your advantage. You don't have to wait for your muse to show up or for inspiration to strike. Try these three tips The next time you feel listless and apathetic.

First, clarify what you want to accomplish. Be precise about your goal, including what you must do to achieve it.

Highlight the reason that fuels your goal. For example, it's hard to get motivated to "lose weight." It's easier to get motivated to "lose 20 pounds by avoiding added sugar so you look good in the summer."

Second, develop a routine that leads to the actions you need to take. Your routine will put you in the right frame of mind. For example, suppose you're a guitarist and writing a song. Your routine might include performing scales and modes, occupying a particular space in your home, and strumming new chords while humming your favorite melodies. Think of your routine as a warmup for the main event (in this case, songwriting).

Third, use time blocks to "plan" your motivation. Put them on your calendar so you won't forget them or allow them to be overridden by other priorities. Commit to doing something related to your goal during these time blocks, even if you're not "feeling it."

Many people think motivation precedes action. But it's the other way around. Action precedes motivation. Once you take action, it becomes easier to *continue* taking action. Your motivation kicks in after you start. For example, imagine you're writing a novel but feel uninspired. The blank page mocks you. The ticking clock on your wall mocks you. Write the beginning of a scene. Write some dialogue. Work on your epilogue. *Do something.* Motivation will follow.

Motivation is a capricious and temperamental ally to self-discipline. But with these tips, you can learn to leverage it. It's worth noting that motivation science is a complex subject, and we've barely scratched the surface. But our coverage will suffice for our goal of cultivating self-discipline and maintaining it throughout your life.

---

1. Chester, D. S., Lynam, D. R., Milich, R., Powell, D. K., Andersen, A. H., & DeWall, C. N. (2016). How do negative emotions impair self-control? A neural model of negative urgency. *NeuroImage, 132,* 43–50.

SELF-DISCIPLINE STUMBLING BLOCKS

~

❝ A stumbling block to the pessimist is a stepping stone to the optimist.

— ELEANOR ROOSEVELT

P eople who claim self-discipline is easy almost certainly misunderstand what it means to lead a disciplined life. Most mistake it for willpower, assuming their ability to resist random temptations makes them disciplined. Some mistake it for motivation, misinterpreting the inspiration they feel in the moment as a sign of discipline.

As you know, neither is true. Worse, these false beliefs

threaten to sabotage any genuine pursuit of self-discipline because they obscure its fundamental principles. If we misconstrue self-discipline, how can we take the proper steps to cultivate it?

The reality is that developing self-discipline and maintaining it for a lifetime is difficult. You're confronted by situations each day that try to undermine your efforts. You're constantly challenged by circumstances that seek to weaken your resolve and tempt you to compromise your goals.

For this reason, it's wise to start this journey by stacking the deck in your favor. This entails recognizing the most common hurdles you'll face and deciding how to handle them. Below, we'll cover the eight biggest stumbling blocks that will imperil your purpose. I'll give you several practical tips on how to clear them.

Stumbling Block #1: Negativity

We're hardwired for negativity. Adverse circumstances have a more significant impact on us than favorable circumstances. Adverse events grab and hold our attention more than positive events (news outlets thrive on this bias). We're drawn to gossip that underscores negativity rather than positivity.

This negativity is an antagonist to self-discipline. Our negative emotions make it difficult for us to behave rationally. We make poor decisions heavily influenced by a skewed outlook, losing control over our impulses and urges.

Spending time with negative people magnifies this problem. Their negativity spreads like a virus, infecting your thoughts, emotions, and attitude. It slowly saps your willpower and kills your motivation.

How to overcome it: First, remove sources of negativity from your life. This includes current event news, rage-bait podcasts and YouTube channels, and people who are persistently gloomy, defeatist, or fatalistic.

Second, focus on the positive side of everything in your life. Practice gratitude for the good things you enjoy. Try to recognize the silver lining in challenging situations. Replace self-recrimination with positive self-talk.

Third, avoid all gossip.

Stumbling Block #2: Unrealistic Goals

We're motivated by goal achievement. Accomplishing something makes us feel capable, competent, and productive. Our success motivates us, improves our self-worth, and gives us a sense of momentum. It encourages us to press forward through any resistance that stands in our way.

Setting unrealistic goals short-circuits this process. Success becomes elusive and even unfeasible. Rather than experiencing small wins and feeling capable, competent, and productive, you experience defeat and feel helpless, inept, and impotent. Staying disciplined is hard when overwhelmed by repeated disappointment and unmet expectations.

How to overcome it: Break down large projects into smaller tasks. Create small, achievable goals to set yourself up for wins.

For example, don't aim to write a novel. Instead, aim to write a chapter. Don't strive to lose 50 lb. Strive to lose one lb per week. Don't set your sights on creating a 7-figure business from scratch. Resolve to make $500 during your first month.

Stumbling Block #3: Undefined Goals

Unspecified goals are as detrimental as unrealistic goals. They're difficult to achieve because they're too vague to be supported by actionable steps. Moreover, monitoring and measuring your progress isn't easy because they're so broad and nebulous. These goals turn into large, intimidating endeavors that eventually seem unachievable. They overwhelm you, slowly wearing down your discipline until you give up.

For example, imagine that your goal is to "get rich." How would you monitor your progress even if you save and invest money each month? How would you know that you're on the right track? How would you know when you've finally achieved this goal? Will you ever feel "rich?"

Because no milestones offer small wins that validate your efforts, you'll never feel as though you're truly making headway. Your motivation and willpower will gradually erode until you give up.

How to overcome it: Set specific goals. Then, work

backward and create distinct milestones to track your progress. For bonus points, attach a reason to your goal.

For example, instead of trying to "get rich," work toward saving $20,000. (Set increasingly higher goals as you complete the one you're working on.) Determine a date for when you'd like to accomplish this goal. Then, create clear mileposts that you can monitor along the way.

Suppose your cutoff date is two years from today. You might save $750 each month, investing the money into a reliable index fund. Each month you do gives you a small win. It's easy to track and will encourage you to stay disciplined in your spending habits.

Give yourself a reason why. For example, you might save money so that you can retire early. Along with the small wins you enjoy each month, this purpose will motivate and inspire you to continue.

Stumbling Block #4: Too Many Options

Having options is usually considered an advantage. But when it comes to developing self-discipline, it's a detriment. The availability of too many options is mentally draining, impairing your decision-making, and exposes you to temptations that may be too difficult to resist. This is the reason recovering alcoholics are advised to avoid bars. It's why recovering addicts are counseled to sever ties with other addicts. The temptation to relapse is too great.

After cultivating self-discipline and the ability to keep yourself in check, having options isn't as dangerous. You can rely on self-control. You can deny your urges consistently and confidently without fear of backsliding into bad habits. But until then, having too many options puts you in a precarious position.

For example, imagine that you're trying to cut sugar out of your diet. You visit the grocery store and walk down the candy aisle, looking longingly at all the delicious treats on display. If your commitment to quit sugar is recent, perusing these choices is dangerous. It's too tempting and increases the likelihood of a relapse.

How to overcome it: Limit your options. While developing self-discipline before you can depend on your willpower and impulse control, avoid situations that expose you to too many choices.

For example, avoid your grocery store's candy aisle if you're on a diet. If you're trying to save money, avoid retail venues unless you *need* to buy something. If you're trying to study and are easily distracted, avoid spaces with foot traffic and multiple noise sources.

Limiting your options in the beginning allows you to practice self-discipline in a controlled environment. As your discipline strengthens, you can reintroduce select temptations to test its stability.

Stumbling Block #5: Identity Tied To Impulses

The way you perceive yourself has a significant influence on your decisions, actions, and behaviors. Research suggests that this self-perception, borne mainly of your past choices, actions, and behaviors, informs and governs your future decisions.[1]

For example, if you've continually surrendered to the temptation of junk food, you'll begin to see yourself as someone who does so. This self-identification makes you more inclined to give in to junk food in the future. It aligns with your self-image.

The influence of self-identity works both ways. If you've consistently resisted the siren song of junk food, you'll start to see yourself as someone who can control this impulse. This makes you more likely to show restraint (research supports this[2]). Again, it aligns with your self-image.

If your identity is tied to any particular urge or vice, it's interfering with your self-discipline. It will continue to be an obstacle until you tame it.

How to overcome it: Adjust your self-image and take small steps toward reinforcing it.

For example, let's say that you want to start exercising and, until now, have led a sedentary life. If you identify as a couch potato, start seeing yourself as someone who exercises. Don't simply aspire to exercise. Create an identity as someone who does it daily.

Then, map out a plan that includes small actions that support this new identity. Your plan might consist of tiny tasks, such as putting on your jogging shoes, stretching, and going for a brisk, 10-minute walk. Easy stuff. But doing these things gives form to your newly-created identity. They become codified as part of your daily routine and, as such, fortify the new manner in which you see yourself.

With this new identity, you'll find it much easier to control your impulses. After all, giving in to them would threaten your self-image.

Stumbling Block #6: Emotional Habits

Throughout your life, you've learned to respond to particular feelings in specific ways. Years of repeated practice have reinforced these responses, turning them into habits. Many of these habits have their roots in your emotional state in the moment.

For example, you may have developed the habit of eating when you feel anxious, procrastinating when you feel dispirited, or scrolling through your phone when you feel unhappy. Maybe you spend money frivolously when you're bored. Or drive recklessly when you're angry. Or behave belligerently when you're fearful.

These emotional habits have become ingrained in your mind. Your behaviors materialize without you having to think about them.

Sometimes, they're helpful. For example, fear can make you more alert to danger and compel you to take action that keeps you safe. However, these habits often make you more susceptible to your impulses. They constitute your brain's way of comforting you when stressed. More specifically, it addresses the cortisol flood that courses through your body when stressed. The main point is that these emotional habits negate your self-discipline. In its attempt to comfort you, your brain encourages you to abandon your impulse control.

How to overcome it: Create new habits that reinforce your impulse control. This is a 4-step process:

1. Sever the link between your negative emotions and their corresponding bad habits (for example, eating junk food when you're anxious).
2. Choose new behaviors to replace the bad habits (for example, performing deep breathing exercises rather than eating junk food when you're anxious).
3. Practice the new behavior whenever the corresponding negative emotion rears its head.
4. Reward yourself for successfully practicing the new behavior in place of the old behavior.

Habit development is a complex topic that demands a deeper dive than above. Treating it in any other manner without acknowledging that would be a disservice. However, it's helpful to recognize the crucial role of habits in cultivating self-discipline. (We'll discuss habits more in *Part II: 10 Steps To Building Self-Discipline*.)

Stumbling Block #7: Present Self Favoritism

I mentioned present bias in the chapter *Why Self-Discipline Is Important*. To recap, it's the propensity to place greater value on immediate than future rewards. It's a universal trait; everyone struggles with it.

This tendency is aggravated by the fact that we favor our present self. We're far more concerned about what we experience in the moment than what we'll experience in the future (ironically, often due to our current actions and decisions). We eat junk food without worrying about health problems down the road. We spend money wastefully without fretting over future financial issues. We drive recklessly without concern about getting into a traffic accident.

Showing self-restraint by controlling our impulses and resisting temptations benefits our future self. Because we prioritize our *present* self, these long-term rewards aren't compelling to us, at least not enough to heavily influence our behaviors. We're *aware* of the potential consequences of our decisions. But we still decide to eat the donut, purchase the latest smartphone, and scroll through social media when we should be working.

This is why developing self-discipline is so tricky, particularly in the beginning. We spend our lives favoring — indeed, *pursuing* — short-term rewards; practicing self-discipline runs counter to years of programming.

How to overcome it: Sabotage your present self's efforts to satisfy its immediate urges.

For example, remove all junk food from your home to

prevent your present self from gratifying its cravings. Start an automatic investment plan to undermine your present self's propensity to spend money irresponsibly. Install a website blocker that stops your present self from wasting time on distracting sites.

As you strengthen your self-discipline, your present self's urges will become less troublesome, and this strategy will become less urgent. But in the beginning, sabotaging your present self can be a pivotal solution to keeping your impulses in check.

Stumbling Block #8: Self-Shaming

Shame can be debilitating. It can paralyze you as you castigate yourself for past mistakes, misbehavior, and perceived shortcomings. It can sap your motivation and cripple your willpower as you fixate on urges and impulses that are shameful to you.

Many people rely on self-shaming to encourage themselves to be disciplined. For example, eating a donut while on a diet isn't just a temporary lapse in judgment; it becomes a source of deep personal humiliation. Buying something frivolous while trying to save money isn't just a fleeting dereliction; it's cause for self-condemnation.

But shame is not an ally of self-discipline. It may seem to support impulse control and self-restraint in the short run, but it always introduces negative emotions. It opens the door to guilt, anger, and depression, fueling the fire. Instead of feeling inspired to pick yourself up, dust yourself off, and do better, you feel more chagrined and dejected.

Shame has an even darker side. Some of our blunders are so embarrassing that we refuse to acknowledge them — to ourselves and others. And if we refuse to admit when we stumble, we can never truly resolve the underlying issues. For example, we never identify the cues that trigger our desperate need to eat junk food. We never figure out why we spend money on frivolous items. Sometimes, our shame is so great that it compels us to disregard our faults because they threaten to demolish how we perceive ourselves.

How to overcome it: Accept that you're going to stumble occasionally. Commit to dusting yourself off when it happens and resuming your journey.

Shame is universal. We all feel it at some level because we all make choices and behave in ways we later regret. It's inevitable, and it's a part of being human. Rather than stubbornly overlooking the things we do that trigger our shame, we should accept them and deal with them head-on. Mistakes may be inevitable, but they're also resolvable. The key to avoiding them in the future is to acknowledge that we make them.

You're going to cave into your impulses occasionally. You're going to falter now and then despite your intentions to the contrary. Your self-control will sometimes flounder. Don't bury the underlying issues or their triggers. Acknowledge them. Accept them. Forgive yourself, and move forward, resolving to do better next time.

This has been a long chapter. But the material we've

covered here is crucial. It's imperative that you're aware of the biggest obstacles that will stand between you and a life of self-discipline. The only way to overcome them is to be familiar with them.

Forewarned is forearmed.

---

1. Fishbach, A., & Woolley, K. (2017). Combatting temptation to promote health and well-being. In *Routledge eBooks* (pp. 167–179).
2. Lee, C., Hochman, G., Prince, S. E., & Ariely, D. (2016). Past Actions as Self-Signals: How Acting in a Self-Interested Way Influences environmental decision making. *PLOS ONE*.

PART II

10 STEPS TO BUILDING SELF-DISCIPLINE

~

In *Part I*, we laid the groundwork. We covered every preliminary item of business relevant to developing self-discipline. In *Part II*, we'll put everything into practice.

This is where the real work begins.

I'll take you through a 10-step procedure for cultivating self-discipline in the following pages. I'll give you every tool you need — and provide tips on how to implement them — to make a personal transformation in this area of your life. By the time you've completed *Part II*, you'll be on your way to successfully controlling your impulses, managing your thoughts and emotions, and making consistent progress toward your goals.

One quick note before we begin: Each section includes

an exercise. I urge you to do them all. They aim to help you apply the tips and advice in the chapters they appear in.

You might be tempted to skip these exercises. Remember that they're simple, easy, and can be completed in minutes. Most importantly, you'll find them helpful. I firmly believe *application* is the heart of developing new habits, routines, and systems. Performing these exercises heeds this principle.

With that out of the way, let's dive into Step #1.

STEP #1: CREATE SMALL, PURPOSEFUL, ACHIEVABLE GOALS

~

❝ Discipline is choosing between what you want now and what you want most.

— ABRAHAM LINCOLN

Everyone has goals. But these tend to be long-term goals. They reflect what people want to accomplish in five, ten years, or even further. Long-term goals are essential because they give us something to aim for. They provide us with purpose and direction.

The problem is twofold. First, they tend to be big and lofty. Second, they're so far off in the distance that they're easy to postpone. Easy to procrastinate. Neither issue supports your journey toward building self-discipline. In fact, long-term goals can undermine it.

For example, imagine that you want to buy your dream home in 20 years. It's a fine, worthwhile goal. But it's so audacious that it's disconnected from your daily experience. Moreover, it's so far off in the future that it's easy to disregard. Neither circumstance is helpful when practicing impulse control and delaying gratification. Neither encourage you to remain committed to your goal.

It's no wonder that failing to achieve long-term goals is practically a cliche. No wonder many people's plans amount to little more than dreams.

But there's a simple solution. And it comes in a small package.

The Power of Short-Term, Attainable Goals

Short-term goals offer three advantages over long-term goals. First, they're achievable. You're not concerned with results that may or may not happen in 20 years. You're driven by what you can accomplish today, tomorrow, or by the week's or month's end.

For example, you're not worried about saving $1 million to purchase your dream home in 20 years. Instead, you're focused on setting aside $300 this month. Or saving $50 *this week* by preparing meals rather than eating out.

The second advantage of short-term goals is that they exist in the present. They compel purposeful action today, tomorrow, and the next day. You're less likely to disregard them because they occupy your headspace here and now.

For example, dismissing a goal you have little chance of achieving in the next several years is easy. It's much more difficult to ignore one for which your actions *today* affect whether you achieve it. You're less likely to procrastinate.

The third advantage is that you receive quick feedback. You quickly know whether your actions move you closer to accomplishing your goal.

For example, suppose that you'd like to lose 50 lb. There's a lot you can do concerning diet and exercise. But it's often hard to know whether your actions are making a difference. It's hard to know whether your actions deliver the best results. But if you focus on losing two lb each week, you'll know almost immediately if your efforts are effective — and you can adjust accordingly.

One of the greatest benefits of setting short-term goals is that achieving them gives you small wins. These wins motivate you to continue. They inspire you to press forward when the going gets tough. They help you build your self-discipline in a way that long-term goals can never match.

A Crash Course on Goal Setting

There's a right way and a wrong way to set small goals. The right way sets you up for success. The wrong way practically guarantees failure. Entire books have been written on this subject. But I'll quickly break down the process here so you can start immediately.

First, determine what you'd like to accomplish. Define it specifically. Be concise. Write it down in a single sentence.

Second, identify the action you'll regularly need to take to achieve your goal.

Third, figure out how you'll know if you're making progress. Your specificity will guide you.

Fourth, work out why you'd like to accomplish your small goal. Know your reason. Know your purpose. (We'll talk more about this in *Step #3: Get Clear on Your Reason Why*).

Fifth, give yourself a deadline. For instance, avoid social media today. Lose two lb by Saturday. Save $200 by the end of the month.

Sixth, identify what you'll need to give up to accomplish your goal. For instance, the instant dopamine hit of scrolling through Twitter or Instagram. The delicious sugar high delivered by junk food. The new pair of shoes you desperately want to buy.

Once you've set your small goals, it's time to put in the work to bring them to fruition. But avoid the trap of single-minded intensity.

Consistency Trumps Intensity

One of my shortcomings is that I get tunnel vision. When I focus on something, everything else fades into the background. This might *seem* beneficial because that type of intensity leads to success, right?

Unfortunately, no.

My tunnel vision imposes many adverse effects. My relationships suffer. I let unrelated tasks fall through the cracks. I miss deadlines. Do I accomplish what I set out to do? Sometimes, but I fail just as often. Ironically, my single-mindedness often leads to failure because I lose track of the bigger picture, including my purpose. Worse, it stimulates my perfectionistic tendencies.

As you might imagine, this does absolutely nothing to strengthen my self-discipline. If anything, it causes my self-discipline "muscles" to atrophy since my actions are largely myopic. I've struggled with this predilection my entire life. While I've managed to get it under control, I encourage you to use me as a cautionary tale.

Consistency is far more important than intensity when working toward your goals. Figure out what you must do, and then do that each day.

You don't have to be perfect. You just need to be consistent. Your consistency will give you momentum. It'll give you opportunities to experience small wins, propelling you forward. The good news is that small goals encourage you to be consistent. They prevent you from feeling overwhelmed. They prevent you from giving up. Instead, they motivate you to continue because the small actions that lead to success are simple and easy and have led to success in the immediate past.

How Self-Compassion Supports Self-Discipline

So what happens if you fail now and again? What do you do if your impulse control breaks down? How should you react to an occasional collapse of your commitment to your goal?

Forgive yourself. Show yourself compassion. Dust yourself off and get back in the saddle.

It's natural to want to be perfect as you work toward accomplishing your goals. But perfection is a mirage. It's an illusion. You're going to make mistakes. You're going to stumble once in a while. When you do, you mustn't beat yourself up. Instead, acknowledge that you're imperfect and will occasionally slip up, but remain committed to your goal.

When you show yourself compassion, you give yourself a chance to renew your commitment. You also allow yourself to recognize that cultivating self-discipline doesn't require perfection. It requires consistency and dedication, both of which are in your control.

∼

EXERCISE #1

∼

THIS EXERCISE HAS TWO PARTS. We're going to create a small goal. Then, we're going to take action toward achieving it.

First, decide on what you'd like to accomplish. Make it specific, concise, and small in scale. An example is to declutter a single room in your home.

Next, establish the action you'll need to take. For example, "discard one item each day."

Come up with a way to track your progress. You may elect to keep written notes. Or cross off days on a calendar after you've taken the action you need to take that day.

Determine why you want to accomplish the goal you created. Keep it simple. For example, you might want to declutter your home office to remove distractions.

Assign a deadline. Make it reasonable without giving yourself too much latitude.

Identify what you'll need to sacrifice to achieve your goal. Lunch out with friends? Your morning latte? Ten minutes each afternoon? Write this down.

Now, the second part of our exercise. Carry out what you need to do each day to make progress toward your goal. Note this action in your tracker.

As you perform this exercise repeatedly, setting and achieving small, purposeful goals will start to feel second nature to you. And the small wins you'll experience will reward you for — and bolster — your self-discipline.

Time required: 20 minutes

STEP # 2: DEVELOP A METHOD TO MONITOR YOUR PROGRESS

∽

" When performance is measured, performance improves. When performance is measured and reported back, the rate of improvement accelerates.

— PEARSON'S LAW

B uilding self-discipline involves trial and error. Some things will work better than others. Some won't work for you at all. Monitoring your results is the only way to know if you're making headway. You must have a way to track the outcome of your efforts. Your tracking system will reveal whether you're on the right track or need to adjust.

The good news is that you've already done most of the work. You've created small goals accompanied by the specific actions you'll need to take to achieve them. Now, we need to build a simple tracker. Before we do that, however, let's quickly review the three biggest reasons.

Three Reasons You Must Track Your Progress

It's possible to succeed without monitoring your results. But you'll be fighting an uphill battle. The brain is adept at maintaining the status quo; tracking your progress short circuits this tendency.

First, your tracking system will keep you accountable. Without it, you may be tempted to cut corners or fool yourself into thinking you've accomplished more than you have.

For example, imagine you've set a goal to lose two lb per week. One of your action steps is to refrain from snacking between meals. If you don't track this action, you might convince yourself that this week's meals were small, so eating a snack today is okay. Without tracking, it's easier to rationalize yielding to temptation.

Second, your tracking system also acts as a prompt. It nudges you to take whatever action you define as integral to achieving your goal.

For example, suppose you want to get into shape. One of

your action steps is to take a 30-minute walk each day. If you neglect to track this action, you may forget to do it. Or you might remember but brush it off because you're "too busy." With a tracker in place, you'll never forget. And if your tracker is in plain sight, you'll be less likely to brush it off.

Finally, your tracking system will motivate you to press onward when you don't feel like doing so. Reviewing each day's success is gratifying. And the longer your string of daily achievements, the more inclined you'll be to extend the string.

For example, let's say that you want to improve your upper body strength. You've decided that one of your daily actions will be to perform 20 pushups each day. If your tracker shows that you've successfully done your pushups 15 days in a row, you'll feel compelled to do them today, if only to maintain the string. It's self-imposed pressure.

Create A Tracking System That Suits You

There are many ways to track your progress, some simple and others elaborate. I prefer simple systems because they pose fewer distractions. Moreover, these days, I rarely monitor anything beyond execution. *Your* tracking system should reflect your tendencies and preferences and the items you want to monitor (more on this in a moment).

Let's start with the simplest type of tracking system: a calendar. In productivity circles, this is sometimes called the "Seinfeld hack." When comedian Jerry Seinfeld was getting started, he wanted to write new material constantly.

He needed a way to keep himself on track. So he hung a huge wall calendar that displayed the entire year via daily boxes. He'd write a new joke each day and use a big red marker to cross off that day on the calendar. The longer the chain of red "X" marks grew, the more pressure he felt not to break the chain.

I love this hack. I've used it throughout my life. But suppose you want a tracker that gives you more flexibility. Let's create one. I recommend doing this on paper in the beginning. Once you've designed a tracking system you're comfortable with, you can transfer it to a spreadsheet. You might even find an app that aligns perfectly with your needs. But let's use pen and paper to start.

First, write down the items you'd like to monitor. You may want to go beyond mere execution. For example, here's a list of potential things to track:

- Your emotions
- Your frame of mind
- Internal resistance (e.g., laziness, self-doubt, etc.)
- External resistance (e.g., distractions)
- Your energy levels
- Time of day you perform your chosen action steps

Next, create a table (on paper) that allows room for you to make notes on each item you'd like to monitor. These notes might be expressed simply as numbers — for example, a "1" for low energy and a "5" for high energy. You don't need much room in that case. Or you may prefer to write a few words — for example, "feeling tired after lunch." You'll need more space in that case.

The most important thing is that your tracking system suits you. Tracking more details provides greater insight but involves more time and effort. Only you can decide where to draw that line. Again, I like to use a simple tracker that monitors execution and nothing else. But initially, I found keeping tabs on the items listed above beneficial.

When to Stop Monitoring Your Progress

There will come a point where your tracking system becomes unnecessary. It will have done its job, helping you to stay on track and delivering helpful insight along the way. But you'll no longer need it. In fact, at that point, continuing to rely on your tracker can do more harm than good. You might find yourself performing actions simply because your tracker reminds you to do them, even if they're less relevant than they were initially.

For example, suppose you commit to reading about a particular subject (e.g., European history in the Middle Ages) for one hour each day. You do this successfully for weeks, noting each day's completion on your tracker. But then you lose interest in this subject. Other priorities become more important to you. You might be tempted to continue reading each day simply because your tracker tells you to do so. In this case, your tracker has outlived its usefulness. It is now distracting you from attending to other matters.

Your purpose essentially becomes overshadowed by your routine.

So, how long should you monitor your progress? There's no universal answer. There's only the answer that best accommodates and complements what you want to achieve. Even if you create an evergreen goal, an objective that is forever (e.g., eat healthy), your tracker will, in time, lose relevance.

It's a terrific instrument for making behavioral changes. For building and reinforcing new habits. For developing self-discipline in areas in which it was previously lacking. But at some point, the changes you make become new routines. New behavioral patterns. At that point, the need to monitor your progress — at least daily — evaporates.

∼

EXERCISE #2

∼

LET'S CREATE A TRACKING SYSTEM. It doesn't have to be perfect. It probably won't be, especially if this is your first attempt. The purpose of this exercise is to build something you can use. Think of it as Progress Tracker version 1.0. You can add features later.

The first step is to brainstorm every metric you want to

track. This can include your emotional state, types of resistance you're struggling with (internal and external), time of day, energy levels, and so on. Write down everything that comes to mind.

You're not committing to tracking them. You're just writing them down so you can review their importance.

Next, choose no more than three metrics to monitor. If you prefer, choose only execution.

Now, try to imagine what your ideal tracking system looks like. The simpler the design, the better (a calendar is the simplest). If you decide to track multiple metrics, you'll need columns. The width of those columns will depend on whether you're using numbers or words. I encourage you to experiment with both to know which suits you best.

You've completed the exercise. You're now armed with a rudimentary tracking system (Progress Tracker version 1.0). You'll probably want to make minor changes while monitoring your chosen metrics.

Time required: 15 minutes

STEP #3: GET CLEAR ON YOUR REASON WHY

~

" The person without a purpose is like a ship without a rudder.

— THOMAS CARLYLE

Have you ever felt stuck regarding your career, relationships, physical fitness, emotional health, or any aspect of life? Have you ever thought you needed to make a change but were unsure what to do? Have you ever felt trapped in an existential limbo and uncertain how to break free?

If so, there's a good chance that you haven't identified your reason why.

The first step forward is recognizing that you need to make a change. (You acknowledge wanting to improve your quality of life.) The second step is to figure out *what* to change. (You decide to work on your self-discipline.) The next step is to determine your reason for making this change.

Your "why" may not be immediately apparent to you. But it's there, fueling your motivation. Below, I'll explain why you need to investigate it, how to discover it, and how to use it to build your self-discipline.

Why You Must Know Why

Having ambitions is easy. Creating goals is easy. Aspiring to be better or improve your life is easy. Taking action consistently to achieve these objectives is difficult. And it's nearly impossible over the long run if your reasons are unclear. Even if you start with plenty of motivation, optimism, and confidence, it's possible (even probable) that you'll give up when you encounter stumbling blocks.

On the other hand, if you have a compelling reason driving you, you'll be far more inclined to persist when the going gets tough.

For example, imagine wanting to lose weight and get into shape. You've decided to improve your health and enjoy the attendant rewards. You feel motivated. Inspired. Ready to get to work.

But then you experience temptations that threaten to deter you. Junk food. Netflix. Video games. Your impossibly comfortable couch. It's a toss-up whether you'll surrender to these temptations if you don't know why you want to improve your health.

That's why you need to know your reason. What is your purpose? What is your motivation? What is compelling you to take action? If you can answer these questions with focus and clarity, you'll find it much easier to resist your impulses and press on.

For example, let's say you want to lose weight and get into shape because doing so will give you the stamina to play with your grandchildren. Or it'll allow you to enjoy outdoor activities with your spouse. These are compelling reasons. They'll sustain you and encourage you to stay disciplined when you might otherwise give up. Your "why" makes you resilient.

How to Identify Your Why

Identifying your why isn't as simple as it seems. Many factors inform your reasons for doing anything in life; some are inconspicuous. They lie beneath the surface, hidden but powerful. Likely, you haven't thought about them for a while. But they influence you nonetheless. And they hold the key to understanding why you feel compelled to change your life.

Your convictions and values play a vital role. Perhaps you feel out of alignment with them and want to course correct.

Your interests also play a role. Maybe you desperately want to learn or improve a particular skill.

Your talents play a role. Perhaps you're unnaturally adept at a specific practice or operation and wish to achieve true mastery.

Your relationships and desire for strong interpersonal connections play a role. Maybe you've noticed that a particular friendship is in serious need of attention.

All of these factors, as well as others, serve as motivation. They give you a reason to stay disciplined when you'd rather give in to temptations. To discover what motivates *you*, ask yourself the following questions:

- What lies at the core of my desire to make a change?
- What is the result that I want to achieve?
- Why do I want to achieve this result?
- What does this situation look like if I successfully make the change I'm considering?
- What does this situation look like if I do nothing?
- What benefits will I enjoy if I make this change? Do they outweigh the costs of pursuing it?
- What consequences will I suffer if I do nothing? Do they outweigh my sacrifices if I decide to move forward?
- Am I excited by the outcome I envision?

- Does the expected result align with my values, convictions, and ideal self-image?

After you've answered these questions, boil your answers down to the following sentence:

I will {insert change} because {insert reason}.

For example…

I will get into shape because I want to play with my grandchildren.
I will save money each week because I want to buy a new laptop to replace my old one.
I will meet my parents for breakfast every Saturday because I want them to know they're important to me.

We're boiling your answers down to a single sentence because doing so keeps things simple. No matter how eloquent, an essay won't compel you to stay disciplined. But a simple statement will. It's clear and concise and will keep you focused on — and moving toward — the outcome you desire. It'll remind you to stay the course when you're tempted to do otherwise.

∾

EXERCISE #3

∾

BECAUSE YOU'RE READING this book, it's a safe bet that you're motivated to develop and strengthen your self-discipline. Now, we're going to discover your "why."

First, select the one area of your life for which becoming and staying disciplined is most important. Maybe it's school. Perhaps it's your career. Or maybe it's a particular relationship that needs attention. Self-discipline will improve your life in numerous ways, but let's focus on just one for this exercise.

Second, write down why this aspect of your life is important. It may be obvious (e.g., "*Of course my spouse is important to me!*"). But maybe it's less evident. If so, writing it down will provide clarity. For example, "*My career is important to me because it funds my lifestyle, improves my self-image, and makes me feel fulfilled.*"

Third, write down the change you're considering, presumably one that requires discipline. For example, "*I'm going to arrive at the office one hour earlier each day.*"

Fourth, answer each of the questions listed earlier. I recommend that you write them down so you can review them easily.

Fifth, create the following statement based on your answers:

I will {insert change} because {insert reason}.

Time required: 20 minutes

STEP #4: LEARN TO MANAGE RESISTANCE

66 Do not be discouraged by the resistance you will encounter from your human nature; you must go against your human inclinations.

— BROTHER LAWRENCE

We face resistance whenever we undertake a task, project, or goal that requires a modicum of self-discipline. This resistance repels us from what we want to accomplish. It tempts us. It distracts us. It derails us. Our success in any endeavor, small or large, often comes down to whether we can act in defiance of this resistance.

Sometimes, the resistance we experience springs from within us. We're affected by our negative emotions, such as fear, sadness, and loneliness. We're overwhelmed by mental stress and catastrophic thinking. Meanwhile, an inner voice criticizes us, telling us we're not good enough and tries to sabotage our intentions.

Sometimes, the resistance we face occurs in our surroundings. Coworkers stop by to chat. Meetings are scheduled that serve little purpose. Our televisions, phones, and refrigerators tempt us. Email, social media, and our favorite websites constantly try to distract us.

Resistance is the obstacle that prevents us from waking up early, sticking to our diets, studying for exams, and working instead of gossiping. It discourages us from cleaning our homes, saving money, and visiting the gym. It thwarts our intentions to read challenging books, manage our time, and control our emotions.

Resistance, whether it originates within us or in our environment, is always at odds with our self-discipline. They run counter to each other. They conflict. So, to cultivate self-discipline, we need to develop viable tactics to push through internal and external resistance.

How to Overcome Internal Resistance

The most effective strategy for dealing with internal resistance is to connect what you want to accomplish with emotional motivation. When your purpose is rooted in your emotions, its influence over you grows. It seems weightier. It becomes more consequential. It suggests a steep price for failure.

Let's return to an example we used in the preceding chapter: You want to get into shape to have the stamina you need to play with your grandchildren. This intention has an emotional component. This is what will encourage you to stick to your plans. If you fail, you might not fully enjoy your time with your grandchildren.

Imagine if your motivation to get into shape was a purely logical one. Getting into shape would decrease your risk of heart disease. It would improve your cardiovascular system. It would boost your immune system. There's no emotional component, which makes these reasons far less compelling. When you experience internal resistance, they're unlikely to help you counter it.

So, establish an emotional motivation for anything you aspire to accomplish. Do you want to lose weight? What is the emotional basis for your intention? Do you want to be more studious? What are the emotional consequences if you fail? Do you want to save money instead of spending frivolously? What negative feelings will you face if you're broke?

Your emotional motivation will be the driving force you need to overcome internal resistance.

How to Counter External Resistance

Countering *external* resistance is mostly about setting boundaries and sticking to them. Some of these boundaries will be entirely personal. They won't affect anyone but you, at least not directly. But some of them *will* affect other people. Maintaining these will require you to be firm and graceful to minimize resentment from others.

An example of the first type of boundary, which only affects you, would be your phone. If it distracts you, turn it off. Or put it somewhere that's out of sight (for instance, in a drawer or cabinet) while you work. Establish that boundary.

Another example is the food in your kitchen or pantry. If you're trying to avoid junk food, remove it from your home. Create that boundary.

Yet another example: your email. If you check your email 30 times per day and want to stop, close your email program and commit to only checking it at 9:00 a.m. and 3:00 p.m. Set that boundary.

What about external resistance involving other people (chatty coworkers, meetings, etc.)? Again, you'll need to set boundaries. But you'll need to do so with attention to finesse and decorum.

An example is the chatty colleague who constantly drops by your office to gossip. You've decided nothing good comes from gossip and want to avoid it. One way to do so is to say you're uncomfortable talking about the individual in their absence. It's firm but civil.

Another example is a significant other who always wants to watch television. You've committed to reading a challenging book and need to be disciplined to do it. You might ask this person, "Would you mind if I read for 45 minutes before joining you to watch Netflix?" You're setting a boundary and doing so with grace.

You'll never get rid of external resistance. You have no control over that. But you *can* minimize their impact by setting reasonable boundaries and sticking to them. And when you communicate these boundaries firmly and courteously, you'll find that most people will respect them.

EXERCISE #4

WE'VE GROWN so accustomed to resistance that we seldom investigate its constituent parts. For example, we know we're often unmotivated but rarely examine the reasons. We recognize that we're dealing with mental stress, but we hardly ever take the time to identify the causes of that stress. We know we're constantly distracted at work but neglect to untangle the individual distractions.

In this exercise, we'll identify and manage these pawns of resistance. Let's start by identifying the factors causing *internal* resistance for you.

First, choose an area of your life where you find it hard to stay disciplined. Maybe it involves your diet or exercise routine. Perhaps it concerns your plan to learn to play a musical instrument. Maybe it involves your desire to remain silent rather than opining about controversial topics on social media.

Second, write down the feelings and emotions compelling you to act in ways that contradict your intentions. For example, imagine you'd like to learn to play the guitar. But when it comes time to practice, you do something else. Is this due to fear? Loneliness? Laziness? Feeling that you'll never succeed? Write it all down.

Third, brainstorm an emotional motivation for your goal. For example, you might want to learn to play the guitar to impress your loved ones. Or maybe you aspire to play live gigs with a band, an experience you're confident will be emotionally rewarding.

You're on your way to overcoming internal resistance. Now, let's focus on the items causing *external* resistance for you.

Again, start by choosing an area of your life where you struggle to control your impulses. For example, suppose you work from home and find it difficult to stay focused and get work done.

Write down every item that distracts you. Examples might include your children, your television, or the internet. They may consist of emails and texts from clients and coworkers, friends who drop by without calling, or your pet who constantly begs for attention.

Next, for each of these distractions, create a reasonable boundary. For example, you might tell your children not to disturb you between 9:00 a.m. and 10:30 a.m. unless there's an emergency. You might decide only to check and respond to emails and texts at 9:00 a.m., 1:30 p.m., and 5:00 p.m. You might ask friends to call before dropping by.

With these boundaries in place, you're prepared to counter all forms of external resistance.

Time required: 20 minutes

STEP #5: CLARIFY YOUR SACRIFICE

～

66 One half of knowing what you want is knowing what you must give up before you get it.

— SIDNEY HOWARD

P ersonal growth of any kind requires sacrifice. This sacrifice manifests in many forms. Sometimes, it involves stepping outside your comfort zone. Sometimes, it entails going beyond your perceived limits of endurance or tolerance. It calls for digging in and refusing to give up. Ultimately, it requires you to forfeit short-term pleasures to reap greater rewards over the long term.

Most of us are taught during childhood that we must "make sacrifices" to succeed in our endeavors. We learn that there's a causative relationship between sacrifice and success. The world-class athlete must sacrifice to remain competitive. The entrepreneur must sacrifice to build a successful business. The high-performing student must sacrifice to earn high marks.

But the nature of this sacrifice, different for each of us, often remains vague. We seldom clarify it. And if we don't know what we must sacrifice to be successful, we can't truly commit to it. Dedicating ourselves to a particular goal is good but not enough. Being willing is noble but insufficient. It's honorable but inadequate.

So, let's look at what you should anticipate giving up to cultivate self-discipline.

What Will Your Self-Discipline Cost You?

This will depend primarily on your goals. The essence and level of your sacrifice will arise from what you're trying to achieve.

For example, imagine that you want to write a novel. Doing so might impose the following costs:

- Relationships (friends and family will miss you)
- Sleep (deadlines are cruel taskmasters)
- Ego (others will critique your work)
- Money (writing precludes earning)
- Hobbies (there are only 24 hours in a day)

Or suppose you'd like to get into shape. You've lived a sedentary lifestyle for several years, so there's plenty of work to do. Staying committed and disciplined might carry the following costs:

- Sleep (you may have to get up early to exercise)
- Your favorite treats (donuts are off the table)
- Social events (birthday parties are risky)
- Personal vices (no more smoking and drinking)
- Time (cooking meals instead of getting takeout)

You must discover what you'll need to give up. By identifying the sacrifices you'll need to make, you'll be better prepared to endure the unavoidable tough times.

For example, suppose your alarm clock goes off at 5:00 a.m. because that's the only time you can exercise. You're tired and groggy. Your vision is blurred. Getting out of your warm bed to drag yourself to the gym requires a Herculean effort. But being aware of this cost in advance makes staying committed to your goal easier. It's still unpleasant. But it's easier to be disciplined.

Is The Sacrifice Worth It To You?

You've identified what you'll need to give up to stay disciplined and dedicated to accomplishing your goal. Now it's time to determine whether you're willing to make those sacrifices.

Put plainly, how bad do you want this?

Some sacrifices might be easy for you. Or at least, they might be easy decisions.

For instance, your doctor might have advised you to quit smoking to live a long, healthy life. Or you might have determined that you need to save money starting today for your child's college education. Giving up a particular vice or forgoing buying a new car may not be easy. But if doing so is a high priority, it's an easy decision.

Other sacrifices are more complex. The decision is more complicated due to the priority of your goal or the nature of the sacrifice.

For instance, suppose you'd like to quit your job and start your own business. Here are some of the things you'll probably have to sacrifice along the way:

- Career
- Sleep
- Income
- Relationships
- Stability
- Watching Netflix
- Social gatherings
- Your health (stress and fatigue take a considerable toll)

Are you willing to give up these things to start a business? Are you ready to sacrifice them, knowing that most new businesses fail?[1] The only way to answer this question honestly is to know precisely what you'll need to give up.

You must clarify the nature and volume of your anticipated sacrifice. Otherwise, you'll find it a monumental struggle to stay disciplined and committed to your goal.

When Your Faith, Planning, and Purpose Converge

In the example above (starting a business), I mentioned the prospect of making sacrifices without knowing whether you'll succeed. This is an important point that deserves a closer examination.

We tend to be optimistic that our efforts in the present will set the stage for success in the future. And to be sure, this optimism is often well-placed. The athlete who practices relentlessly competes at a higher level. The student who studies continuously gets higher marks. The dieter who avoids junk food loses weight.

But sometimes, the future is less predictable. It's less reliable. There's a possibility that practicing self-discipline in the present may not produce the outcome you desire.

For example, imagine you're committed to saving money for your child's college education. With that objective in mind, you forgo frivolous purchases and invest monthly into mutual funds. But let's say the economy struggles, and the mutual funds fail to produce the returns you need to meet your financial goal. Imagine how difficult it would be to stay disciplined given these regrettable circumstances.

Your faith, planning, and purpose will encourage you to remain committed when you're tempted to give up.

They'll help prevent negative emotions from causing you to abandon your discipline.

For example, despite your mutual funds' disappointing returns, you still have faith in the stock market. You know that the stock market has steadily grown over the last 100 years and is likely to continue growing. Meanwhile, your plan to invest each month, a form of dollar-cost averaging, remains a sound strategy, particularly as the market fluctuates. Finally, your purpose hasn't changed. You still intend to fund your child's college education.

These three elements — your faith, planning, and purpose — serve as tentpoles for your self-discipline. They fortify your impulse control, temperance, and dedication to your goal and help you to weather outcomes that fail to meet your expectations. By reminding yourself of their validity, you'll find it easier to stay the course, confident that your sacrifices remain sensible.

∼

EXERCISE #5

∼

THIS EXERCISE IS SIMPLE, quick, and easy. Grab a pen and pad of paper.

First, choose one goal you'd like to achieve.

Second, brainstorm things you'll need to give up while you pursue this goal. Write them down. Take your time.

The items you'll need to sacrifice may not be immediately apparent.

Finally, review your list. For each item you've written down, ask yourself the following two questions:

1. "Am I willing to give this up to achieve my goal?"
2. "Am I willing to give this up if success isn't guaranteed?"

There's no shame in discovering that a particular sacrifice is too big. The important thing is that you're aware of the sacrifices ahead of time and, armed with this insight, can make pragmatic decisions about whether you should move forward.

Time required: 10 minutes

---

1. Delfino, D. (2023). The percentage of businesses that fail — and how to boost your chances of success. *LendingTree*. https://www.lendingtree.com/business/small/failure-rate/

STEP # 6: USE THE 10-10-10 RULE

❝ Your biography is not your destiny; your decisions are.

— TONY ROBBINS

Self-discipline is usually discussed in the context of temperance, resilience, and persistence. These attributes indeed occupy its core. But when you strip them away, self-discipline, at its most basic level, comes down to decision-making. Your decisions ultimately define and demonstrate your ability and willingness to delay gratification. To show self-control. To stick to your goals.

Each day, you're put in situations that require you to choose between competing options. You either stay committed to your plans or give in to urges and temptations. Giving in entails abandoning your plans, at least temporarily.

By this point, you've set specific, achievable goals and determined what you'd like to accomplish. You have a clear image in your head of your ideal future self. To cultivate the skills, habits, and improvements your ideal future self embodies, you'll need to make numerous decisions, beginning now.

The "10-10-10" rule is a valuable tool to help you make decisions that align with your goals.[1] This tool will encourage you to stick to your plans when you're teetering between staying committed and giving in to your impulses.

The 10-10-10 Rule Explained

We often make decisions emotionally. This, in and of itself, is neither good nor bad. Our emotions are a fundamental part of who we are. They're essential to our humanity.

But our emotions favor the present. They focus on what is happening *right now* and advocate the quickest path to feeling better. This is the reason many people eat junk food when they're feeling stressed. It's why some folks lash out at others when they're enraged; it's akin to releasing a pressure value.

Allowing your emotions to dictate your decisions will lead to regrettable situations. The 10-10-10 rule resolves this problem by extending your perspective and encouraging you to use reason to dilute the potency of your emotions. Here's how it works:

Whenever you face a choice between sticking to your plans or surrendering to your impulses, ask yourself the following three questions:[2]

1. How will I feel about my decision in ten minutes?
2. How will I feel about my decision in ten hours?
3. How will I feel about my decision in ten days?

If you give in to your urges and pursue immediate gratification, abandoning your self-discipline, you might feel fabulous in ten minutes. But in ten hours, after you've gained some distance from the decision, you'll probably experience regret. And in ten days? You might even admit, "Well, *that* was a terrible decision."

For example, imagine that you're trying to stay away from junk food. But in apparent sabotage, someone has brought a box of donuts to the office. Donuts are your favorite treat, and you now have a choice to make.

If you abandon your self-discipline and eat a donut (or three), you might feel gratified in ten minutes. But in ten hours, you may feel differently after reconsidering your decision in light of your goal. Regret might have set in by this point. And in ten days, when you're still struggling to control the urges triggered by that fateful decision? You

DAMON ZAHARIADES

might admit to yourself in shame, "Self, that was a huge mistake."

The 10-10-10 rule encourages you to consider these feelings ahead of time. It allows you to avoid the regret and shame that poor decisions might elicit.

How the 10-10-10 Rule Encourages Self-Discipline

The 10-10-10 rule expands your frame of reference. It compels you to adopt a longer-term viewpoint when you're tempted to cater to your emotions in the present.

Sometimes, your emotions are so potent, and the impulses they promote are so powerful that you need distance from them. You need this distance to regain your perspective. To stay disciplined and committed to your goals and intentions when every fiber of your being pushes you to do otherwise.

Your emotional self seldom recognizes the future consequences attached to present decisions. It wants what it wants, and it wants it *now*. If it acknowledges consequences, it disregards them, figuring it will deal with them later. By prioritizing the present, your emotional self encourages impulsiveness.

The 10-10-10 rule short-circuits this tendency by lengthening your point of view. It forces you to consider the soundness of your decisions from the perspective of your ideal future self. It compels you to ask yourself, "Given what I want to achieve, and in light of who I want to be, am I making the right choice?" It encourages you to

122

use reason and sound judgment to temper your emotions and remain in control.

The Power of Present-Future Continuity

Present-future continuity is a fancy way of saying that the more connected you are to who you want to be, the more likely you'll make decisions with the latter in mind. Let's unpack this.

We've already discussed your ideal future self. This is the person you envision becoming. This persona embodies the goals you want to accomplish, the qualities you hope to personify, and a fusion of all the skills, habits, and attitudes you wish to adopt.

Your present self is you at this very moment. This persona fixates on your present needs, worries, and immediate impulses. It favors instant gratification and advocates decisions, actions, and behaviors to achieve it.

Your present self is naturally at odds with your ideal future self. It's not worried about the future. It's concerned about the here and now. It cares neither about who you are nor what you're struggling with three months from today. It cares about *today*.

The good news is that you can train yourself to connect these two personas. You can modify your frame of mind so your present self and ideal future self work together to help you stay disciplined. You can do this by associating your present actions with short-term and long-term rewards.

For example, suppose you're trying to avoid eating junk food again. Your purpose is to lose weight and get into shape. You have an image of your ideal future self (yes, you look fantastic!). But your present self doesn't care about this image. It doesn't care whether you achieve it. Your present self wants to know, "What's in it for *me*? Why should *I* give up junk food?"

So, you associate the actions you aspire to take (i.e., giving up junk food) with both immediate and future rewards. The future rewards should already be evident since you determined your reason why in *Step #3*. The immediate rewards might include the following:

- Mental clarity
- Better sleep
- More energy
- Easier digestion
- Improved mood

You've given your present self a compelling reason (five reasons, in fact) to stay away from junk food. These are rewards your present self can experience today. Because of this, it's now more inclined to make decisions that help you to realize your ideal future self. That encourages you to stay disciplined and in control.

You've achieved present-future continuity.

There are plenty of studies that demonstrate this effect.[3456] They're worth reading if you want to dive deeply into this fascinating aspect of psychology. For our purposes, it's enough to recognize the effect exists and understand how to take advantage of it.

~

EXERCISE #6

~

First, choose a goal you'd like to achieve. It should require self-discipline daily.

Second, identify a single action that's imperative to achieving this goal.

Third, identify a decision that opposes this action.

Fourth, apply the 10-10-10 rule.

Lastly, connect the action of your present self to the attainment of your ideal future self.

Let's go through an example together…

Goal: Lose ten lb.

Action: Avoid junk food.

Opposing decision: Eat a donut.

The 10-10-10 rule applied:

1. How will I feel about this decision in ten minutes?
2. How will I feel about this decision in ten hours?
3. How will I feel about this decision in ten days?

Present-future continuity: Avoid junk food so that I feel

better, think more clearly, and enjoy better quality sleep starting today. Avoid junk food so I can lose ten lb.

These two personas are now in alignment. That'll help you to control your impulses, stay disciplined, and stick to your plan.

Time required: 10 minutes

1. The 10-10-10 rule was developed by Suzy Welch, former editor-in-chief of the *Harvard Business Review*.
2. Welch's original 10-10-10 rule uses longer timeframes: ten minutes, ten months, and ten years. I've adopted shorter timeframes that are more suitable for our purposes.
3. Rutchick, A. M., Slepian, M. L., Reyes, M. O., Pleskus, L. N., & Hershfield, H. E. (2018). Future self-continuity is associated with improved health and increases exercise behavior. *Journal of Experimental Psychology: Applied, 24*(1), 72–80.
4. Ersner-Hershfield, H., Garton, M. T., Ballard, K., Samanez-Larkin, G. R., & Knutson, B. (2009). Don't stop thinking about tomorrow: Individual differences in future self-continuity account for saving. *Judgment and Decision Making, 4*(4), 280–286.
5. Reiff, J., Hershfield, H. E., & Quoidbach, J. (2019). Identity over time: perceived similarity between selves predicts Well-Being 10 years later. *Social Psychological and Personality Science, 11*(2), 160–167.
6. Hershfield, H. E., Cohen, T. R., & Thompson, L. (2012b). Short Horizons and Tempting Situations: Lack of Continuity to Our Future Selves Leads to Unethical Decision Making and Behavior. *Organizational Behavior and Human Decision Processes, 117*(2), 298–310.

STEP #7: EMBRACE DISCOMFORT THROUGH TRAINING

66 You have power over your mind — not outside events. Realize this, and you will find strength.

— MARCUS AURELIUS

Humans are naturally averse to discomfort. We avoid it whenever possible. Given a choice between being comfortable and uncomfortable and all other variables remaining the same, we'll always choose the former. It's hardwired into our DNA.

But what if discomfort is the key to our self-growth and self-discipline? What if exposing ourselves to discomfort in various forms builds our resilience? What if consistent, controlled exposure can improve our ability to control our impulses, resist temptations, and persist when things get tough?

The fact is, discomfort is everywhere, and it's never going away. We'll never rid ourselves of it entirely. But we can learn to embrace it, at least in small doses. And if we manage to do so, we can use it to train ourselves to remain committed to our goals regardless of our circumstances. To stay dedicated to our plans irrespective of our impulses and temptations. To continue being steadfast in our intentions despite our indecision and laziness.

In other words, we can exploit our discomfort and use it to strengthen our self-discipline. The first step is to adjust our expectations.

Adjusting Your Expectations

We learn at a young age that life isn't fair. Certainly, our perspective may be skewed if our parents regularly accommodated us during our formative years. (Cue pre-teens crying, "That's not fair!" when told they have to wait to buy the latest smartphone.) But we eventually discover that life involves discomfort.

As we mature, we learn that comfort is only guaranteed if we do nothing. And even then, it's fleeting; it erodes while we're in stasis. Feeling entitled to lasting comfort inevitably leads to disappointment and frustration.

So we must adjust our expectations. We must acknowledge that we don't have a right to feel comfortable. We don't control every aspect of our circumstances. Bad things can — and often do — happen to us despite our meticulous planning and honorable intentions. So, we must grow comfortable with being *uncomfortable*. At the very least, we must recognize that discomfort is inescapable.

Moreover, you can expect to feel uncomfortable if you aspire to do anything beyond your comfort zone. If you hope to break out of your status quo, expect to face inconvenience, unpleasantness, and even mild distress. Growth is always accompanied by discomfort. If this weren't so, self-improvement would be easy and without struggle.

Now that we have the right expectations let's use discomfort to our advantage.

Resistance Training For Your Self-Discipline Muscles

Resistance training increases strength and endurance in physical exercise by applying force or weight against your muscles. An example is lifting a dumbbell. The weight of the dumbbell works against the contraction of the muscle fibers in your bicep. Through repetition, this resistance leads to muscle growth.

Your self-discipline muscles work similarly. When you use them to resist urges and temptations, they become stronger. The more you use them, the stronger they become.

For example, suppose you've started to eat healthy and avoid junk food. You've probably noticed that the longer you stick to a healthy diet, the easier it gets. Likewise, imagine you've trained yourself to wake up at a particular time each morning. You've probably noticed that the longer you do this, the less inclined you are to hit the snooze button and sleep in.

These are examples of resistance training for your self-discipline muscles. You've decided to do something outside your comfort zone (e.g., eat healthy, wake up early, etc.). Doing it is uncomfortable in the beginning. Each time you do it, you apply resistance to this new "muscle." The more you do it, the stronger this "muscle" becomes; eventually, the thing that was once outside your comfort zone is now within it.

You can use resistance training to strengthen your self-discipline in nearly any context. Dieting, exercising, writing a book, studying for an exam, doing household chores, learning to play an instrument, being punctual, and so on.

Start small by applying a *little* resistance. For example, if you usually wake up at 8:00 a.m. and want to be an early riser, don't immediately start waking up at 4:30 a.m. Get up at 7:45 a.m. each morning for a few days. Then, start setting your alarm for 7:30 a.m. Then, aim for 7:15 a.m. Give your self-discipline muscles time to develop. As they grow, apply more resistance until you've accomplished what you set out to do.

Interval Training For Your Self-Discipline Muscles

Interval training puts your muscles to use for a set period and a set number of repetitions. An example of the former would be sprinting for five minutes. An example of the latter would be lifting a dumbbell 15 times. Like resistance training, interval training builds strength and endurance. However, it relies on short bursts of activity to develop muscle fibers.

As with resistance training, we can use interval training to build our self-discipline muscles. This works best for incorporating practices requiring extended action or attention (or both).

For example, imagine that you want to write a novel. But you're finding it challenging to plant yourself in a chair before your keyboard. You'd rather watch television, play guitar, or hang out with friends.

One way to use interval training is to commit to sitting in front of your keyboard for 15 minutes. It'll be uncomfortable. The impulse to do other things won't magically disappear. But that's what this training is for — to strengthen your self-discipline muscles.

After five minutes, give yourself the freedom to do something else, even if you haven't written a single word of your novel. When you're ready, return to your chair for another 15-minute interval. Do this until it's no longer uncomfortable.

Then, extend your writing interval to 30 minutes. You'll probably feel uncomfortable again. When the discomfort dissipates, extend your writing interval to 45 minutes. Continue this process until you've reached your desired interval, and sticking to it is no longer uncomfortable.

~

EXERCISE #7

~

LET's reinforce what we've just covered with a quick exercise.

First, choose an action you'd like to make part of your daily routine. Select one that requires you to apply yourself for an extended period. Maybe you'd like to write a novel as in the example above. Or perhaps you want to start jogging, reading non-fiction, or practicing the piano. Whatever action you choose, identify how it will make you uncomfortable.

Next, use resistance training to adopt this action into your routine. For example, let's say you decide to read non-fiction each evening. If you seldom read non-fiction, doing so will be uncomfortable when you start. Tolerate the discomfort. Press through it and resist the temptation to do other things (e.g., watch television).

Third, use interval training to lessen the discomfort attached to your chosen action. For example, commit to reading non-fiction for 15-minute intervals. When this becomes comfortable for you, commit to 30-minute intervals. Over time, you'll develop the discipline to read non-fiction for periods that may have seemed unimaginable.

Time required: 10 minutes (to create a plan)

STEP #8: TURN ACTIONS INTO SYSTEMS

~

66 If you do something every day, it's a system. If you're waiting to achieve it someday in the future, it's a goal.

— SCOTT ADAMS

I n *Step #4*, we talked about internal and external resistance. We discussed how both threaten to sabotage your plans. Both try to convince you to give in to your impulses rather than practicing temperance and self-control.

In *Step #7*, we examined the discomfort that always accompanies self-improvement. Whenever you aspire to do something, expect to experience discomfort. It's unavoidable.

These obstacles and the sacrifices you're making to stick to your plans (for more on sacrifices, see *Step #5*) mean that staying disciplined requires a great deal of willpower. That's problematic because willpower is steadily depleted as the day progresses. It's impossible to maintain for long periods. Therefore, we can't rely on it to stay disciplined. We need another option.

Enter systems.

Systems are a series of actions. They are routines that signal to your body and mind that it's time to do something specific. You can do these things with minimal thought or effort when they become habitual.

For example, imagine you're getting ready for bed in the evening. You brush your teeth, create tomorrow's to-do list, pray or meditate, read a book, and perhaps do a few stretches. This is your evening routine. It's your evening *system*. You don't have to think about doing the individual actions. None of them require any willpower. They're part of your system, and it's easy to stay disciplined in doing them.

Systems Always Trump Willpower

In 2011, the American Psychological Association (APA) published the results of its annual *Stress in America* survey. Among the APA's findings were the following:

> Almost everyone (93 percent) surveyed reported making a resolution to change some aspect of their behavior in 2012. Yet people consistently report that a *lack of willpower is the top reason they fall short of their goals* to lose weight, save more money, exercise or make other life-style changes.[1]

We've examined the shortcomings of willpower, so this finding isn't surprising. Moreover, it's safe to assume nothing has changed since then. Most people continue to depend on willpower despite its limitations.

Systems trump willpower in two ways. First, they alleviate the need to rely on a finite, depletable resource. If you rely on willpower, how can you possibly remain disciplined to do what you need to lose weight, save money, or exercise when it's gone?

Second, willpower is unsteady because it's closely tied to your emotions. It rises and falls based on how you feel at any given moment. It's fickle and, therefore, unpredictable.

When you develop and follow systems, these issues evaporate. You no longer need to worry about having enough willpower to stay disciplined. Your systems ensure that you remain disciplined. Once they become part of your routine, you don't have to think about it.

Systems Remove the Need for Constant Motivation

Motivation is as unreliable as willpower, though for different reasons.[2] Recall the last time you didn't "feel motivated" to do something. There's a good chance that something never got done. (Or it was addressed after a lot of procrastination.)

Motivation can be helpful when it gives you energy and inspiration. These feelings invigorate you and spur you to take action. The problem is that they're inconsistent and short-lived. That burst of energy and inspiration dissipates quickly. Once it's gone, so too is the compulsion to take action.

Systems remove the need to feel motivated. You no longer have to rely on feeling energized or inspired to take action. Your system signals your body and mind that it's time to act. The only thing you need to do is show up.

Let me illustrate with a personal example. Writing isn't always easy for me. Sometimes, it's a struggle. But if I want to publish, I have to write. I must be disciplined enough to write daily.

If I were to rely on willpower, I'd write a little each morning, but not in the volume needed to publish. If I were to rely on motivation, I'd write sporadically. That would be a problem, too.

So, I created a system for myself. Each morning, after I get out of bed, I drink two glasses of water, pray, do a few stretches, and read for five minutes.[3] After I've completed this routine, I'm ready to write. My body and mind have gotten the message. And the writing happens regardless of whether I have a full tank of willpower or feel motivated.

Systems Silence Your Inner Critic

Your inner critic thrives on uncertainty, indecision, and procrastination. Whenever you attempt to do something challenging, or that lies outside your comfort zone, and you hesitate, your inner critic will try to sabotage you. It is very good at its job.

This negative voice in your head will try to convince you that you're incompetent, unskilled, or unprepared. It'll whisper that you're not good enough, not smart enough, and not committed enough. Give your inner critic an inch of latitude, and it'll wreak havoc with your self-discipline.

When you create and stick to systems, uncertainty or indecisiveness no longer hamper you. Nor are you delayed by procrastination. You know what you need to do and when you need to do it. Your systems dictate your actions. These actions happen with minimal thought and effort, and your inner critic loses its foothold.

It may continue to speak negatively, but its voice becomes desperate and pathetic. Easy to ignore. Easy to silence.

~

EXERCISE #8

THIS EXERCISE IS NOT ONLY quick and easy but also fun. We'll create a system you can follow when you're not motivated or inspired.

First, choose a task you need (or want) to complete daily. Completing this task should require discipline. Here are a few examples:

- Complete homework
- Write in your morning journal
- Write a novel
- Exercise
- Read non-fiction
- Practice playing the guitar
- Learn a new language
- Meditate

Next, brainstorm a series of actions that might precede this task. These actions *can* be related to it, but they don't have to be.

For example, suppose you want to write each morning toward completing a novel. Your system might appear like this:

1. Drink a cup of coffee
2. Meditate for five minutes
3. Do 20 pushups
4. Go for a 10-minute walk

5. Listen to Chopin for five minutes
6. Sit in front of your keyboard
7. Review your outline

If you follow this system consistently each morning, you'll find that sitting down to write becomes easy. You don't have to think about it. You don't have to possess willpower to make it happen. Your system will prepare your mind and body to do what you need to do when needed.

Time required: 10 minutes

---

1. *What Americans Think of Willpower: A Survey of Perceptions of Willpower & Its Role in Achieving Lifestyle and Behavior-Change Goals.* (2012). American Psychological Association. https://www.apa.org/topics/stress/willpower.pdf
2. Refer to the chapter *Self-Discipline vs. Motivation* to revisit this discussion.
3. Sometimes, I read material that is related to what I'm writing about. But often, I read completely unrelated non-fiction.

STEP #9: MINIMIZE AND MANAGE STRESSORS

∽

66 If you ask what is the single most important key to longevity, I would have to say it is avoiding worry, stress and tension. And if you didn't ask me, I'd still have to say it.

— GEORGE BURNS

S tress can be useful in certain circumstances. It prompts the fight-or-flight response when your safety is threatened. In short bursts, it spurs you to take purposeful action, motivating you to do what's necessary to achieve your goals.

But stress can also significantly and seriously affect your

mental and physical health. Repeated bouts of acute stress (e.g., traffic jams, arguments with your spouse, demanding deadlines, etc.) will make you irritable, ruin your focus, and negatively impact the quality of your sleep. Chronic stress (e.g., money problems, a pending divorce, a severe illness, etc.) can cause you to experience anxiety, persistent headaches, and depression. It can even expose you to heart disease.[1]

None of these effects are conducive to self-discipline. On the contrary, they erode your discipline, making it more difficult to control your impulses and delay gratification. You undoubtedly know this from experience.

Once you've mastered self-discipline, you'll find it easier to keep yourself in check during stressful times. But in the beginning, stress will be an obstacle when you're developing your discipline muscles. Worse, it will likely be insidious and creep up on you.

For this reason, while you build your self-discipline, you'll need to take preemptive measures to minimize and manage the stressors in your life. I'll give you several practical tips for doing so below. But let's first look at how the stress response works.

How the Stress Response Works

When your mind perceives an external threat, it reacts to keep you safe. This survival mechanism starts in the brain, which sounds the alarm and processes and interprets information about the perceived threat. Your brain triggers the release of cortisol and adrenaline, which prepare your mind to make quick decisions and your body to take single-minded action.

This process was remarkably effective at keeping our ancestors safe. Back then, life was filled with danger, and the fight-or-flight response played a vital role in staying alive and well.

Today, however, the stress response poses problems. It can still be useful but often misidentifies emergencies. It sometimes perceives threats to your safety where no threats exist. It puts you on high alert when you don't need to be and unnecessarily releases a flood of stress hormones. It does so in reaction to everyday stressful events.

For example, imagine sitting in traffic while running late. You're going to miss an important meeting. Your heart starts beating more rapidly; your breathing becomes shallow; your concern about missing the meeting turns into anger. Meanwhile, the ocean of red brake lights in front of you fuels your irritation and anxiety.

This is your stress response in action. Not only is it stimulating a primal reaction, but the reaction is both unnecessary and impotent. The traffic jam isn't life-threatening. And you can't do anything about it anyway, so you're left to stew in your stress.

Your stress response places you in these types of emotionally intense situations over and over as it repeatedly misidentifies emergencies. The more often this happens, the more difficult it is to keep yourself in check.

How Stress Affects Willpower

Exerting willpower and self-control requires a lot of mental energy. When faced with options that promise to gratify your immediate urges, you try to make wise decisions that align with your goals. This occurs repeatedly throughout the day, sapping your energy each time.

Acute and chronic stressors also require a lot of mental energy. As we noted above, your brain puts you on high-alert status, demanding on-the-spot attention from you. This, too, occurs over and over throughout each day.

The problem is that practicing willpower — and, in a broader sense, self-discipline — is at odds with your brain's response to acute and chronic stressors. Both are focused on achieving completely different ends.

When you exert willpower, you do so to accomplish long-term outcomes. For example, you exercise to protect your health as you age. You push yourself to write your novel because you envision publishing it next year. You reject a coworker's flirtations because you want to preserve your marriage.

When your brain responds to stress, it focuses on short-term outcomes. For example, you rage at a traffic jam because it's making you late for a meeting. You skip lunch to meet a tight deadline that afternoon. You frantically cram to pass an impending exam at school.

These two processes conflict. They work at odds with each other. But because the stress response has such a powerful physiological effect, it steals the mental energy you need to exert willpower. If you experience continual stress, this response can completely overwhelm your ability to control your impulses and remain committed to your goals.

So, let's consider practical ways to reduce your life's acute and chronic stressors.

Practical Tips To Manage Stress

The following suggestions may or may not work for you, depending on your circumstances. A few might seem perfectly tailored to your situation, while others seem irrelevant. The broader point to recognize is that you likely possess the power and influence to manage your stressors and minimize their effects on you.

Question your perception of the stressor — If something is causing you stress, ask yourself why. Does your situation truly require your immediate attention? Is it as urgent as it seems? Or is your brain sounding the alarm unnecessarily? For example, suppose you have an exam tomorrow. Perhaps you're prepared despite your brain putting you on high alert.

Delegate tasks — If your workload is unrealistic, ask yourself whether you must be responsible for every item on your to-do list. Can you delegate things? Can you outsource them? Do this in the office (maybe a coworker can take a task or two off your plate). Do this at home (maybe your children can take a chore or two off your plate).

Change your environment — A toxic workplace is highly stressful. A toxic living space is equally stressful. Ask yourself whether you must remain in these environments. Can you get a job where your bosses and coworkers are more supportive? Can you change your living situation to get away from bad roommates or manipulative family members?

Practice mindfulness meditation — Meditation gets a bad rap. But that's mostly because many folks misunderstand it. They imagine a person sitting with crossed legs and hands outstretched with thumbs and index fingers touching. Maybe there's a gong in the background — maybe trickling water — maybe whispered mantras. The fact is, there's a considerable body of research that suggests mindfulness meditation relieves stress.[234]

Make self-care a high priority — Maintain a healthy diet. Get sufficient sleep. Exercise daily (leisurely walks count!). Review your emotions regularly. Tell your inner critic to take a hike. It's easy to disregard these simple things, especially when life gets hectic. But they work. I can tell you from experience that they alleviate stress.

Make new friends — Isolation and loneliness are stressful. If you're feeling isolated and lonely, try to meet new people. Volunteer your time at a pet shelter. Join a local book club. Take a cooking class. Strike up a conversation with someone who frequents your favorite coffee shop. This is easier said than done, especially if you're an introvert. But all it takes is one new friend to see life in a different light.

Talk to someone you trust — Some stressors are grave, urgent, and persistent. For example, someone close to you may have passed away, you might have lost your job, you're going through a contentious divorce, or you're suffering from a significant injury or illness. You don't have to remain silent. You don't have to maintain a tough exterior. Talk to someone. A trusted friend. A beloved family member. A licensed and experienced therapist.

We've spent so much time discussing stress in this chapter because it has a debilitating, ruinous effect on self-discipline. Once you successfully manage the stressors in your life, you'll find it much easier to exert impulse control and go the distance when you're tempted to quit.

∿

EXERCISE #9

∿

WRITE down five current stressors in your life. They could be acute or chronic. They can be related to your career or your home life. They can involve other people or something you're dealing with alone.

Next, brainstorm one thing you can do starting today to alleviate the stress imposed by each of the five stressors. Just one.

For example, let's say your morning commute stresses you out. You might try breathing exercises. Or leave your home ten minutes earlier. Or listen to an inspiring audiobook.

Suppose you're lonely, and that's causing you stress. Commit to saying hello to one stranger this afternoon. At the grocery store. At your favorite coffee shop. At a local park.

The purpose of this exercise isn't to relieve the stress you're feeling. Instead, it encourages you to brainstorm simple, proactive steps to alleviate stress. It's designed to help you recognize that you have plenty of control, perhaps more than you realize.

Time required: 10 minutes

---

1. Satyjeet, F., Naz, S., Kumar, V. K., Aung, N., Bansari, K., Irfan, S., & Rizwan, A. (2020). Psychological stress as a risk factor for cardiovascular disease: a Case-Control Study. *Cureus*.
2. Tang, Y., Hölzel, B. K., & Posner, M. I. (2015). The neuroscience of mindfulness meditation. *Nature Reviews Neuroscience, 16*(4), 213–225.
3. Khoury, B., Lecomte, T., Fortin, G., Masse, M., Therien, P., Bouchard, V., Chapleau, M., Paquin, K., & Hofmann, S. (2013). Mindfulness-based therapy: A comprehensive meta-analysis. *Clinical Psychology Review, 33*(6), 763–771.
4. Kogias, N., Geurts, D. E. M., Krause, F., Speckens, A., & Hermans, E. J. (2023). Study protocol for a randomised controlled trial investigating the effects of Mindfulness Based Stress Reduction on stress regulation and associated neurocognitive mechanisms in stressed university students: The MindRest study. *medRxiv (Cold Spring Harbor Laboratory)*.

STEP #10: FORGIVE YOURSELF WHEN YOU STUMBLE

66 You forgive yourself for every failure because you are trying to do the right thing.

— MAYA ANGELOU

Your journey toward mastering self-discipline won't be a smooth one. You'll experience ups and downs, successes and failures. Sometimes, you'll unwaveringly keep your impulses in check while giving everything you have to the task before you. And you'll celebrate those triumphs. Other times, you'll stumble, indulging in laziness and choosing immediate gratification over your goals. And you'll feel regret.

This is entirely normal. Everyone goes through this process as they work to improve themselves. It's part of the journey. Everyone makes mistakes. Everyone experiences failure. Everyone feels regret.

But not everyone forgives themselves.

When you stumble, practice self-compassion. Instead of beating yourself up, let yourself off the hook. Be willing to pardon yourself.

This doesn't mean you should ignore or disregard your regrettable decisions and behaviors. Nor should you make excuses for them. On the contrary, it's important to recognize your setbacks so you can figure out why they happened and learn from them.

Your Mistakes Are Learning Opportunities

We make mistakes for many reasons. Sometimes, it's a lack of self-awareness. We don't fully appreciate our weaknesses and overestimate our capacity for resisting temptation. For example, we mistakenly eat a single piece of chocolate, believing we can refrain from eating additional pieces.

Sometimes, it's due to stress. We're under pressure and succumb to the temptation to experience relief (*hello, chocolate!*). Our willpower is exhausted, and we haven't developed systems to do the heavy lifting in staying disciplined.

Sometimes, it's an error in judgment. For example, we give ourselves less time than we need in the morning before work. We end up feeling rushed and not in control. So we make regrettable decisions ("*I don't have time to make breakfast, so this donut will have to do.*")

The problem isn't that we make mistakes. Again, that's normal. The problem is that we make the same mistakes over and over. The actual obstacle is our refusal to learn from them.

All mistakes are learning opportunities. Once we're willing to acknowledge them — indeed, to *own* them — we can look for the lessons they offer us. We can determine why we made the mistakes and brainstorm measures to avoid repeating them.

This process makes us feel empowered as we can now take proactive steps to pursue and effect the future outcomes we desire. It also makes us more inclined to forgive ourselves because we focus on moving forward.

Your Failures Are Learning Opportunities

Many people perceive failure as a reason to give up. They take action that falls short of their hopes and expectations and concede defeat. For them, failure isn't a stepping stone to success. It's justification for abandoning their goals and aspirations.

On the one hand, this is understandable. Failure is discouraging. Sometimes, it's emotionally painful. And when others witness it, it can be embarrassing. It's easier to call it a day than persevere and risk failing again.

On the other hand, doing so is a missed opportunity. If we reframe and investigate our failings, they become useful to us. They can give us insight into aspects of our lives that need attention.

For example, imagine that you aspire to jog each morning but repeatedly fail to do so. Rather than abandoning your goal, assuming you'll never achieve it, investigate the possible reasons behind the failure. For instance, perhaps you're…

- Getting insufficient sleep
- Waking up too late
- Hitting the snooze on your alarm
- Uncertain *why* you want to jog each morning
- Fatigued due to a poor diet

Once you've identified the problem, you can take steps to resolve it. You can decide to go to bed earlier. You can wake up 20 minutes earlier and refuse to hit the snooze on your alarm. You can clarify your reason for jogging. You can improve your diet to enjoy more energy.

Going through this process elicits the same effect as going through it when we make mistakes. We feel empowered to take corrective action. And because we're focused on moving forward, we're inclined to forgive ourselves rather than punish ourselves.

Failing Doesn't Make You a Failure

You may feel compelled to attach your mistakes and failures to your self-image. You might feel as if they are representative of your worth. If you have habitually castigated yourself for such things in the past, this association might happen naturally. It might even seem intuitive to you.

You must sever the connection between your mistakes and failures and how you perceive yourself. You are *not* your mistakes. You are *not* your failures. And neither are indicative of your resolve, values and convictions, or capacity to learn and improve.

The road to developing self-discipline is a long one. And it's fraught with snares and enticements that continuously attempt to lure you off the path. You'll occasionally stumble. You'll capitulate to your urges from time to time. You'll make mistakes now and then.

Don't chastise yourself. Don't shame yourself. Instead, show yourself compassion and empathy. Forgive yourself. Acknowledge that failing doesn't make you a failure; it moves you closer to achieving what you set out to accomplish. The key is to seek insight into your decisions and behaviors.

∼

EXERCISE #10

∼

WRITE down three instances in the recent past where you made a mistake that contradicted your intentions.

For example, you might have eaten a candy bar despite

intending to avoid junk food. You may have decided to hang out with friends, knowing you should study for an upcoming exam. You might have chosen to watch television instead of going to the gym.

Review each of the three situations. One at a time, ask yourself why you made that particular decision. For example, maybe you ate the candy bar because you skipped lunch and felt hungry. Maybe you hung out with your friends because you were feeling lonely. Perhaps you chose Netflix over visiting the gym because you had zero energy.

Next, sever the connection between these decisions and your self-image. Acknowledge that you made a mistake and remind yourself that mistakes are inevitable. The important thing is that you avoid repeating them. And this leads us to this exercise's final step.

Determine ways to counter the reasons that compelled you to make your decisions. For example, you might eat lunch daily to avoid feeling hungry and seeking a sugar rush.

When you commit to seeking insight and moving forward instead of wallowing in regret and shame, you'll immediately be more willing to forgive yourself for missteps.

Time required: 15 minutes

BONUS STEP #1: MAKE YOURSELF ACCOUNTABLE TO SOMEONE

66 Most people fail not because of a lack of desire but because of a lack of commitment.

— VINCE LOMBARDI

We discussed the merits and mechanics of tracking your progress as you build self-discipline (for more on this subject, see *Step #2*). Your tracking system allows you to monitor your progress and keep yourself accountable... to yourself. This is an indispensable step.

But there's something uniquely helpful about making yourself accountable to another person. You're making a profound commitment when you share your goals and aspirations with someone and describe precisely what you intend to do to achieve them. This type of commitment will motivate and inspire you in ways that personal accountability alone can't and won't.

The Power of Accountability

Being accountable involves taking responsibility for your actions and decisions. It means accepting that you, and *only* you, are answerable for your results. Success or failure, you're in charge. The buck stops with you.

When you make yourself accountable to another person, you make this individual a part of your team. They'll root for you. They'll encourage you. And they'll hold your feet to the fire if you don't produce your desired results.

The right accountability partner will help you to stay on track. They can help you to identify and break through roadblocks. They'll encourage you to be honest with yourself when you stumble and celebrate your small wins.

Your accountability partner is your companion, confidante, consultant, and support team, all wrapped into one. Having this person in your corner will embolden you to give everything you have and do whatever is necessary to accomplish your goals.

Levels of Accountability

At a bare minimum, your accountability partner should check in with you to ask whether you're on track. This might involve a simple text asking, "Did you do XYZ today?" It could entail a quick phone call during which you describe the actions you've taken. It may involve a 5-minute Zoom meeting during which your partner reminds you of self-imposed deadlines and checkpoints.

This is a valuable arrangement. And it may suffice for your needs. But there's even greater benefit in committing to a higher level of accountability.

For example, you might want your partner to ask you for a detailed progress report each afternoon. This would include the actions you've taken and the problems you faced. Your accountability partner can ask you questions that help you identify these problems and develop ways to avoid or resolve them in the future.

Or your partner can help you to sift through your emotions and help you to identify the behaviors that are attached to them. For example, do you eat junk food when you're angry? Do you skip your daily workout when you're stressed?

The partnership and accountability you forge with your partner is entirely up to you. You get to design both in a way tailored to your temperament and needs.

How to Find a Suitable Accountability Partner

Your accountability partner can take many forms. They might be a trustworthy and reliable friend. They could be a former coach who inspired and encouraged you. They might be a mentor with whom you're currently working. They could be a former business partner or current coworker. Or your "partner" could take the form of a local support group or an online community of folks with similar goals.

The individual (or group) you choose will occupy a crucial position. They're going to play a decisive role in your success. So you'll want to choose wisely. Here are a few practical tips:

First, your partner should be unbiased. They need to bring objectivity to the arrangement. You don't want someone who will commiserate with you. Your partner should be willing to bring attention to actions and behaviors that contradict your intentions (without being judgmental).

Second, your partner should have your respect and confidence. For example, they might have already mastered self-discipline, making you hope they can help you emulate their success.

Third, your partner should make you feel comfortable being vulnerable to them. Remember, you'll share your mistakes and failures with this person, along with your small wins and big successes. You must be able to share the former without fear or shame.

Take your time in choosing a suitable accountability partner. The care you show upfront can make the difference between selecting someone who helps you and someone who ends up doing more harm than good.

EXERCISE #11

THERE ARE two steps to this exercise. First, describe the type of accountability arrangement you prefer. Be specific.

Would you like this person to check in with you via text message once a day? Or would you rather schedule a twice-daily meeting on Zoom? Do you want your partner to ask for confirmation that you've completed specific tasks and exercises? Or would you favor a more in-depth inquiry?

Remember, you can design any arrangement you desire. Moreover, you can modify it along the way. The most important thing is that your arrangement suits you. It should inspire and encourage you to stay on course.

The second step is to select an accountability partner. This is best done on a sheet of paper.

Consider everyone in your life who has been a healthy source of motivation. Write down their names. Review each one and ask yourself whether the individual has ever challenged your decisions or behaviors in a supportive manner. Have they ever graciously "called you out" for doing something that opposed your stated goals and ambitions? If the answer is no, draw a line through that name.

Your ideal accountability partner will be among the remaining names on your list.

Time required: 15 minutes

BONUS STEP #2: CREATE A REWARD/CONSEQUENCE SYSTEM

66 No person is free who is not master of himself.

— EPICTETUS

Earlier, we discussed how developing self-discipline is easier when we create systems that guide our actions and behaviors (for more on this subject, see *Step #8*). These systems and routines encompass individual habits that are performed in sequences. Building these systems requires that we develop the habits that underlie them.

In 2012, author Charles Duhigg published *The Power of Habit*, describing the "habit loop." Duhigg says this loop regulates establishing and adopting practices that become part of our norm. It helps to shape both good habits and bad habits.

This habit loop is composed of three components:

1. A trigger that prompts the behavior
2. Our response to the trigger
3. The reward for the response

While all three components are essential, we're going to focus on the third one. Rewards hold a significant influence over us. They motivate us to behave in specific ways. They influence our decision-making process. And if we implement them correctly, they'll become a handy tool for strengthening our self-discipline.

We can't discuss the beneficial effects of rewards without discussing the impact of consequences. Both are potent. Both influence our behaviors and decisions. The question is, are they equally effective in cultivating discipline?

Reward vs. Consequence: Which is More Effective?

Rewards and consequences are often discussed in the context of positive and negative reinforcement, respectively. But this is an overly simplistic way to think about them. It ignores complexities we must acknowledge before creating a functional reward/consequence system.

We're hardwired to think of positive as "good" and

negative as "bad." But, we need to adjust our perspective when using rewards and consequences to encourage or discourage certain behaviors. We need to consider positive as "adding something" and negative as "removing something." In this context, both can be used to reinforce and penalize.

Let's consider "positive" first. Imagine that you want to lose weight, and you decide to give up junk food. Positive reinforcement might come as permission to go to the theater. You're adding the promise of an experience to reward your desired behavior (avoiding junk food). Positive *punishment* might come in the form of cleaning the bathrooms in your home. You're adding an experience to penalize giving in to your urges.

Now, let's consider "negative" using the same goal. An example of negative reinforcement would be the removal of Brussels sprouts from your diet (or pick any vegetable that makes you instinctively cringe). You're removing something you detest to reward your discipline. An example of negative *punishment* would be restricting your internet browsing. You're eliminating something you enjoy to penalize a lack of discipline.

In this context, rewards and consequences can be equally effective. Both can play important roles in shaping your behavior. Both can motivate you to keep yourself in check and go the extra distance when tempted to give in or give up.

How to Create a System Tailored to You

You must determine what motivates you to build a productive, reliable system of rewards and consequences. What prompts you to act? What encourages you to behave in specific ways? You must find the rewards you select to be sufficiently desirable. Similarly, the consequences you choose should be adequately unpleasant.

No system will be effective without follow-through. Reward yourself if you successfully remain disciplined when you're tempted to do otherwise. If you fail to maintain your discipline, penalize yourself. If you don't follow through consistently, the promise of rewards and consequences will become meaningless. When this happens, they'll no longer influence you.

Specify precisely how you'll reward or penalize yourself. For example, suppose your reward for staying disciplined is to visit the cinema. Select the film you intend to watch. Choose the showtime. Suppose your penalty for lacking discipline is to restrict your internet browsing. Specify the duration (e.g., 45 minutes). Designate the period (e.g., 7:00 p.m. until 7:45 p.m.).

Keep your rewards and consequences separate from one another. For example, if your reward is to visit the cinema, your consequence shouldn't be to skip the cinema. Conversely, if your penalty is to restrict internet browsing, your reward shouldn't be to allow internet browsing. Removing rewards you've already earned will discourage you and make you cynical. Removing consequences that have already been applied will dilute their influence and make them seem meaningless.

Lastly, avoid choosing overly severe consequences. You should find them unpleasant enough to influence your behavior but not so draconian that they smother your motivation.

~

EXERCISE #12

~

THIS EXERCISE IS VERY SIMPLE. First, write down three things that you enjoy doing.[1] Your list might include visiting the cinema, eating a particular treat, or meeting a friend for coffee.

Second, write down three additional things you enjoy doing and would miss if you were prohibited from doing them. This might include playing video games, reading for pleasure, or watching television.

Prohibiting the activities on your second list involves negative punishment. You can also use positive punishment. Examples include forcing yourself to do 50 pushups, clean your bathrooms, and donate money to a charity you dislike. I prefer to use negative punishment. It's what works for me. But your system should be tailored to *you*.

Lastly, don't cross-pollinate your two lists. Keep your rewards and consequences separate.

Time required: 10 minutes

---

1. I recommend using experiences as rewards rather than purchased goods for three reasons. First, you'll have more flexibility in rewarding your small successes. Second, buying things isn't consistently satisfying. The allure quickly wears off. Third, you'll save money.

BONUS STEP #3: IDENTIFY A ROLE MODEL

~

❝ We tend to become like those we admire.

— THOMAS MONSON

Except for finding an accountability partner (for more on this topic, see *Bonus Step #1*), your journey to becoming disciplined has been a private one. You've relied on your motivation, willpower, and inspiration. You've created goals and developed systems that depend on no one else. You've counted on your capacity and resolve to overcome challenges.

Now, you're going to look outward. You're going to look for a role model.

If you're an individualist at heart, finding a role model might go against your nature. You're used to doing things on your own. Looking to someone else for guidance and inspiration will seem unnatural to you. But you'll likely benefit from doing so. The individual you choose can help you overcome common obstacles, conquer recurring difficulties, and galvanize your efforts when you're tempted to give up.

How Role Models Help Shape Your Identity

You've had role models in your life, even if you're independently minded. You looked to your parents during childhood, whose actions informed your own. Your friends and classmates influenced you in school. As a young adult entering the workforce, you may have admired a coworker who seemed exceptionally knowledgeable, proficient, and influential.

These role models served a variety of purposes. They gave you a jumping-off point when you weren't sure how to get started. They exemplified attributes associated with the success you wished to emulate. They demonstrated habits that gave rise to and even accelerated that success.

These individuals inspired you, showing you what was possible despite the roadblocks in your path. They motivated you to achieve *more* and refuse to give up when tempted to throw in the towel. They encouraged you to take calculated risks despite your uncertainty and fear.

No role model is perfect, of course. They made

mistakes like everyone else. But that, too, was to your benefit. Witnessing their mistakes and observing how they
bounced back from them shifted your frame of mind. You
began to perceive mistakes as learning opportunities rather
than a source of nagging regret and shame.

Plainly put, the people you've looked up to throughout
your life, even subconsciously, have helped shape your
identity. They've played a role in defining who you are,
including your values, convictions, and aspirations.

A role model can be a valuable ally as you build self-
discipline. Of course, the key is choosing the right individual for the job.

How to Find a Suitable Role Model

Choosing someone who already typifies or possesses what
you want to achieve is tempting. For example, you might
pick a wealthy person if your goal is financial discipline.
You might choose someone who appears healthy if your
goal is physical discipline. You might select someone who
seems calm, confident, and even-tempered if your goal is
emotional discipline.

But if you don't know *how* these people accumulated
wealth, achieved physical fitness, or developed emotional
control, you cannot know if they're suitable role models.
You can't know what character traits, if any, led to their
current circumstances. Or even if their circumstances are
what they seem.

For example, maybe the wealthy person is the beneficiary of an immense trust and is a spendthrift rather than financially disciplined. Perhaps the person who appears healthy struggles with unseen health problems stemming from multiple vices. Maybe the individual who seems calm and confident is good at suppressing his rage.

With that in mind, here's a quick cheat sheet for choosing a suitable role model. The person you select should:

- Regularly demonstrate impulse control
- Maintain personal and interpersonal boundaries
- Follow routines that support their intentions
- Perpetually develop good habits
- Have a history of correcting bad habits
- Show unwavering commitment to their goals
- Know why they want to accomplish their goals
- Be methodical (e.g., use to-do lists)
- Be decisive
- Be aware of their weaknesses
- Always meet deadlines (self-imposed or not)
- Be willing to answer your questions regarding their success

If you've identified these attributes in someone, you've found a suitable role model.

Can A Negative Role Model Help?

A negative role model is a person who embodies traits that you want to curb or reverse in yourself or avoid developing in the first place. This person represents an outcome you want to circumvent. They are a cautionary tale of what can happen if you follow in their footsteps.

 People focus on role models; it is more effective to find antimodels – people you don't want to resemble when you grow up.

— NASSIM NICHOLAS TALEB

For example, imagine (again) that you'd like to get into shape. To accomplish this goal, you commit to exercising daily and eliminating junk food from your diet. A negative role model would be someone who maintains a sedentary lifestyle and eats donuts, sweets, and sugary drinks. As a result of these choices, this individual might struggle with weight-related issues, sleep apnea, lack of energy, and even serious health problems like diabetes.

In their way, a negative role model can inspire and motivate you. They typify circumstances that you want to avoid.

EXERCISE #13

WRITE down the names of everyone you know who seems disciplined. Consider friends, family members, coworkers, neighbors, and acquaintances. Note the decisions they've made and the actions they've taken that make them seem disciplined to you.

Next, use the cheat sheet above to determine whether each person on your list would make a good role model. Take your time. Rushing this process and making a hasty choice will do more harm than good. Cross out the names that fail to qualify.

You should now have a short list of names remaining. Choose one.

Brainstorm five questions you'd like to ask this individual regarding their discipline. For example, you might ask about their process for setting and sticking to boundaries. You might ask how they create good habits and correct bad ones. You might ask them to describe their most significant obstacles in developing discipline and how they overcame them.

Approach this person. Ask them if they're willing to answer a few questions. Be upfront about your intentions. Be ready to suggest and willing to schedule an appointment if they're busy.

Time required: 30 minutes

YOUR SELF-DISCIPLINE ACTION PLAN:
A 60-SECOND RECAP

~

W e've covered a lot of material and completed over a dozen exercises. Hopefully, we've gained actionable insight about ourselves along the way. Let's take a moment to catch our breath and quickly recap what we've learned.

Step #1: Create Small, Purposeful, Achievable Goals

Long-term goals are essential. But when it comes to building self-discipline, short-term goals are even more so. They give you feasible targets to hit in the present. And they give you quick feedback regarding whether you're on the right track. You're less likely to put them on the back burner and more likely to take action.

Step #2: Develop A Method To Monitor Your Progress

To paraphrase a quote often credited to management consultant Peter Drucker, "You can't improve what you don't measure." Regularly monitoring your progress makes you feel more accountable for your actions and decisions. This personal accountability spurs you to take action and make decisions that support your intentions.

Step #3: Get Clear On Your Reason Why

Intentions without purpose are impotent. You won't be truly committed if you don't know why you want to achieve something. If you know why, you'll be compelled to go the distance when you're tempted to give up and admit defeat. It'll motivate you to resist your immediate impulses to enjoy greater rewards down the road.

Step #4: Learn to Manage Resistance

You're going to face resistance as you build and improve your self-discipline. Both internal resistance (e.g., negative emotions) and external resistance (e.g., environmental distractions) will pose obstacles. Overcome the former by connecting your purpose with some emotional motivation. Counter the latter by setting and maintaining boundaries.

Step #5: Clarify Your Sacrifice

Cultivating self-discipline requires sacrifice. You must know what you'll give up to remain dedicated. You must understand what building self-discipline will cost you, now and in the future. Once you've identified the nature of the sacrifice, ask yourself whether you're genuinely willing to make it. This shapes and reinforces your commitment.

Step #6: Use the 10-10-10 Rule

Your emotions prioritize the present over the future. They'll happily give your urges and impulses free rein since that's the quickest path toward gratification. The 10-10-10 rule urges you to adopt a longer-term perspective regarding abandoning self-discipline. It temporarily restrains your emotions so you can make rational, purposeful decisions that align with your goals.

Step #7: Embrace Discomfort Through Training

Discomfort is inescapable, particularly when trying to achieve something that demands focus and effort. Rather than avoiding it, which is impossible, embrace it. First, adjust your expectations regarding whether you'll experience it (you most certainly will). Then, use resistance and interval training to improve your resilience.

Step #8: Turn Actions Into Systems

You can't count on willpower or motivation to keep yourself in check and go the distance when you want to give up. Both are fleeting and, therefore, unreliable. Systems and routines are superior. Once they become habitual, they'll do much of the heavy lifting for you.

Step #9: Minimize and Manage Stressors

Stress is an antagonist to self-discipline because it stimulates an emotional response (remember, your emotions favor the present). Even though stress is a part of life, not all stressors are necessary. Minimize the pointless stressors and manage the inescapable ones to reduce their cumulative effect on you.

Step #10: Forgive Yourself When You Stumble

It's not a question of whether you'll stumble. The question is *when*. Everyone makes mistakes. Everyone makes regrettable decisions. When this happens to you, show yourself compassion. Forgive yourself and look for lessons in your mistakes. If you regard your mistakes and unfortunate decisions as learning opportunities, you'll feel more inclined to stay committed to your goal.

BONUS STEP #1: Make Yourself Accountable To Someone

Accountability encourages ownership. You feel more responsible for your behaviors and decisions when you have to answer for them. The right accountability partner can help you stay on course and identify roadblocks while serving as your cheering section. But choose this individual carefully.

BONUS STEP #2: Create A Reward/Consequence System

Rewards and consequences encourage and discourage desired and undesired behaviors (respectively). Determine what motivates you and what you find to be disagreeable. Using this insight, create a tailor-made system of rewards and penalties that inspires you to stay disciplined.

BONUS STEP #3: Identify A Role Model

It's possible to master self-discipline without looking to others for inspiration. But if you can shorten your path to mastery by observing their paths, why not do so? A good role model can provide a veritable roadmap to success, including avoiding mistakes and how to recover from them.

PART III

HOW TO STAY DISCIPLINED FOR A LIFETIME

~

Cultivating self-discipline is the first leg of your journey. It's arguably the most important leg, but it's only the beginning. Like any skill, self-discipline must be practiced regularly to keep it sharp. Like a muscle, it must be exercised repeatedly to maintain its strength.

It's okay if you only want to develop discipline to occasionally achieve short-term goals (e.g., lose 15 lb, study for a final exam, etc.). But if you'd like to master self-discipline to draw upon it whenever you need it, your work isn't done.

In fact, your work is never truly done.

Keeping yourself in check — mentally, physically, and emotionally — gets easier with practice. But it's never *easy*.

Staying committed to your goals may seem simple, but that's mostly because you've implemented systems that support your intentions. Digging in and giving everything might feel natural, but that's because you've trained yourself to go the extra distance.

It doesn't happen naturally. It takes effort and vigilance.

Bottom line: If you want to remain disciplined for the rest of your life, you must continually exercise your self-discipline muscles. You must practice temperance, impulse control, and self-denial over and over. You must periodically stress-test your willingness to push through discomfort and go the extra distance when tempted to throw in the towel.

So, let's turn your self-discipline into a habit.

CREATING YOUR SELF-DISCIPLINE HABIT

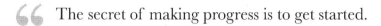 The secret of making progress is to get started.

— MARK TWAIN

I n the section *Common Misconceptions About Self-Discipline*, we noted that no one is born with self-discipline. It's something we learn about, decide to adopt, and labor to improve. We all start at the same place: as infants, we possess zero self-control. We develop it later in life (or choose to give free rein to our impulses).

This is good news because we don't have to rely on innate ability or natural talent. Self-discipline isn't a skill that some can cultivate, but not others. It isn't a trait that some can develop, but others must do without it. Each of us can build, strengthen, and eventually master self-discipline.

Mastery takes more than effort. It takes diligence. It takes continual practice. It takes perpetual commitment. We must regard self-discipline as more than just a skill or ability. We must perceive it as — and turn it into — a life-long habit.

New Habits Require Repeated Application

You've undoubtedly heard that forming a new habit takes a specific number of days. For example, cosmetic surgeon Maxwell Maltz claimed in his book *Psycho-Cybernetics* that doing so takes 21 days. Researcher Dr. Phillippa Lally authored a study that suggested it might take anywhere from 18 to 254 days.[1] Many people claim that 30 days marks the ideal threshold, but that's probably because it fits nicely on a calendar.

Let's ignore how long it takes. Instead, let's focus on the more salient lesson: If you want to create a self-discipline habit, you must regularly execute the related actions.

For example, let's say that you'd like to get into the habit of drinking eight glasses of water each day. You must train yourself to reach for a glass of water when you usually reach for coffee, soda, or a sugary energy drink. The only way to make this work — the only way to make it *habitual* — is to do it repeatedly.

Or let's suppose you're a student and your grades are

slipping because you're not spending enough time studying. You have to train yourself to study when you might prefer to watch television or browse social media. The training only sticks if you do it again and again.

Small Steps Produce Remarkable Results

You might be tempted to build self-discipline by creating large goals fueled by ambitious activities. Don't do this. It usually leads to failure, disappointment, and frustration. Failed New Year's resolutions, which tend to be big and bold, are practically a meme.

Instead, build self-discipline with baby steps. Maintain a consistent pace rather than rushing forward with an aggressive plan. Focus on incremental improvement instead of explosive leaps forward.

Pick one small, achievable goal and devise little actions you can take to accomplish it. For example, let's say that you decide to exercise every day. Here are some small steps you can take:

- Go for ten-minute walks
- Do ten pushups, sit-ups, or squats
- Take the stairs each morning at the office
- Vacuum one room in your home

You get the idea. These are small activities that require very little time. Moreover, they're so simple and easy that it's difficult to justify *not* doing them.

And here's the most important point: doing them over and over makes them a part of your routine. They become *habitual*. They begin to feel like second nature, so *not* doing them seems strange. This is the secret to creating a self-discipline habit. It's also the secret to making the habit stick.

And the best part? Over time, small actions taken consistently produce impressive results. For example, losing one lb each week means losing more than 50 lb during one year. Reading ten pages of non-fiction each evening means finishing a book each month.

Developing self-discipline isn't about setting grandiose goals and making radical action plans. It's about the tiny things you do regularly that gradually improve your impulse control, grit, and fortitude.

Face Your Stumbling Blocks Head On

One last note before we get to this section's exercise. We discussed stumbling blocks in *Part I*. And we talked about internal resistance in *Part II* (for more on resistance, see *Step #4*). Many people ignore these things, at least in the beginning. For example, they regularly procrastinate but refuse to acknowledge their tendency to do so. Or they often spend money on frivolous items but purposefully overlook this behavior.

Ignoring our personal obstacles and weaknesses slows our progress in developing our self-discipline habit. If we put off confronting them, they'll remain unresolved and continue to get in our way.

If you recognize a hurdle, face it head-on. Don't ignore it. Don't put it on the back burner to deal with it later. Address it immediately. Investigate the reason you do it and come up with simple steps you can take to curb the tendency.

For example, if you want to start jogging but tend to procrastinate, commit to putting your jogging shoes on. Then, do this whenever you feel like delaying jogging. If you want to save money but often spend impulsively, commit to delaying purchases for 24 hours.

Bottom line: Face your stumbling blocks as soon as you recognize them. There's a good chance they're easier to resolve than you imagine.

∼

EXERCISE #14

∼

CHOOSE one small goal that you'd like to achieve. (Use the crash course on goal-setting we covered in *Step #1*.)

Next, identify three simple and easy actions you can take each day to move closer to achieving this goal. The less time they require, the better. Note that for this exercise, we're not concerned about the outcome. We're focused on the *process*.

Finally, schedule these three things each day. Don't leave them to chance. Don't merely put them on your to-do list. Find a spot for them on your calendar. You might even assign all three to a single time block.

It's now a simple matter of addressing them daily at their allotted times.

Time required: 10 minutes

---

1. Lally, P., Van Jaarsveld, C. H. M., Potts, H. W. W., & Wardle, J. (2009). How are habits formed: Modelling habit formation in the real world. *European Journal of Social Psychology*, *40*(6), 998–1009.

REINFORCING YOUR SELF-DISCIPLINE HABIT

∽

66 In reading the lives of great men, I found that
the first victory they won was over themselves... self-discipline with all of them came
first.

— HARRY S. TRUMAN

Throughout this book, we've likened self-discipline
to a muscle. It grows stronger when you use it.
And it atrophies when you don't use it.

To extend this analogy, your muscles need ongoing
maintenance. Daily physical activity helps you to maintain

muscle mass. Similarly, practicing self-discipline daily helps you to maintain impulse control and resilience.

Now that you've developed your self-discipline habit, it's important to reinforce it. Otherwise, it'll wither, and all your invested time and effort will be wasted.

Fortunately, reinforcing these "muscles" can be done easily. It just requires a little planning. And, of course, once your plan is in place, you'll need to show up consistently.

The Power of Small Experiments

Many of our goals are ambitious and wide-reaching. We want to run a marathon, learn a second language, or be a better parent or spouse. We want to earn a degree, get into shape, or buy our first home.

It's important to have big long-term goals. But they won't help us to reinforce our self-discipline habit. At least not until we break them down into much smaller goals. Once we break them down, we can run experiments to "stress test" our self-discipline muscles.

I call them experiments because some will bear fruit while others won't. Both outcomes are acceptable for our purpose. The important thing is that we run them regularly. Doing so exercises our self-discipline muscles, providing them with the ongoing maintenance they require.

Here's an example:

Let's suppose you'd like to get into shape after years of living a sedentary lifestyle. That's a big goal that'll take a long time to achieve. But hidden inside that goal are numerous smaller ones. If you break down the bigger goal, you'll have no shortage of experiments you can run to reinforce your self-discipline. For instance, you can...

- Forgo the sugary snack you have after lunch
- Perform ten pushups each morning
- Go for a 15-minute walk after breakfast
- Stand and stretch every 30 minutes
- Prepare breakfast instead of grabbing a pastry
- Cook dinner instead of getting takeout
- Drink two glasses of water upon waking up

This is the tip of the iceberg. There are countless experiments you can run. Again, the outcome isn't that important in the context of our purpose. Even if these experiments fail to produce your desired results, they'll still reinforce your self-discipline. The mere act of regularly doing things that counter your impulses bolsters it.

These small experiments don't necessarily need to be attached to your long-term goals. They can be entirely self-contained. Here are a few examples you might try over one week:

- Give up coffee
- Refrain from buying anything you don't need
- Avoid all foods with added sugar
- Forgo watching TV until 9:00 p.m.
- Don't browse the internet until 5:00 p.m.

- Keep your phone off until noon
- Read non-fiction for 30 minutes
- Write in a journal for 30 minutes
- Study an online course for 30 minutes

These are just a few ideas to inspire you to brainstorm your small experiments. The key is regularly doing things that oppose your natural tendencies and urges.

Schedule Your Discipline Experiments

Like any habit, the best way to ensure that you reinforce your self-discipline habit is to schedule the related tasks (or, in this case, experiments). When you schedule them, you're less likely to skip them. The tasks become part of your routine, like brushing your teeth before bed. Once they're a part of your routine, doing them regularly becomes an afterthought.

If you don't schedule your experiments, they're likely to get pushed aside by more urgent tasks. The busier life gets, the more value we place on our spare time. When life becomes chaotic, we find it easier to justify skipping experiments. So schedule them to remove that temptation.

Experiments accompanied by times of the day don't need to be scheduled. For example, if you decide to refrain from browsing social media until 5:00 p.m. each day this week, you don't have to put it on your calendar. Time is baked into the experiment.

Other experiments should be scheduled. For instance,

if you commit to reading non-fiction for 30 minutes, create a 30-minute time chunk and put it on your daily calendar. Block off that time, and you'll be inclined to use it exclusively for reading.

Reward Yourself For Small Wins

We talked earlier about the habit loop as detailed by Charles Duhigg (for more information on this, see *BONUS STEP #2*). Recall that reward is one of the three essential pieces of this loop. When developing any habit, the reward serves two purposes. First, it provides motivation.

Second, it helps the brain to remember the loop. The more frequently you act in a manner that produces a reward, the less internal resistance you'll face when taking that action in the future.

Come up with a small reward that you can give yourself for completing the experiment you choose to undertake. Ideally, this reward will gratify a longing or desire you have.

For example, imagine that you successfully read non-fiction for 30 minutes today. You might allow yourself to spend ten minutes browsing social media as a reward. This would indulge your hankering to keep up with your favorite social media site. Meanwhile, and more importantly, it would motivate you to continue the experiment, reinforcing the loop of your self-discipline habit.

∾

EXERCISE #15

BRAINSTORM ten small experiments you can do daily over one week. These might reflect and support your long-term goals (e.g., forgoing your favorite sugary afternoon snack to get into shape). Or they might be self-contained experiments (e.g., giving up your morning coffee).

I've found the best way to do this is to identify a personal vice and devise an experiment that opposes it. For example, I watch a lot of YouTube videos that analyze films. So, I might forgo YouTube until 8:00 p.m. That requires discipline (for me).

Next, come up with a small reward for successfully doing each experiment each day. For example, my reward for forgoing YouTube until 8:00 p.m. might be watching two videos analyzing films I enjoyed.

I recommend conducting one experiment at a time, at least initially. Think of it like visiting the gym for the first time. You don't want to spend three hours doing every exercise and using every piece of equipment. That's a good way to hurt yourself. Instead, start with baby steps. As your self-discipline habit grows, continue to stress test your "muscles" by doing multiple experiments simultaneously.

Time required: 20 minutes

MANAGING YOUR SELF-DISCIPLINE HABIT

66 The flame that burns twice as bright burns half as long.

— LAO TZU

We've spent most of our time together talking about how to delay gratification and go the extra distance when we're tempted to give up. Our purpose is to achieve our long-term goals and aspirations. We deny our immediate impulses to enjoy future benefits.

That's self-discipline in a nutshell.

But it's possible to go too far. With single-minded

resolve, we can become so committed to achieving our long-term goals that we sacrifice too much in the present. We forfeit our quality of life *now* to improve our quality of life *later*.

Extreme self-discipline may seem fruitful and respectable (even virtuous), but it imposes an exorbitant cost. Despite the future benefits it can produce, it's a recipe for regret.

The Danger of Too Much Self-Discipline

You probably know someone who works too much. This individual puts in 80+ hours a week, working nights and weekends. They rarely take vacations. They work when they're sick. If they have a spouse and kids, they rarely see them.

On the one hand, this individual appears disciplined. How else can we explain their intense commitment to their work and the sacrifices they continually make? On the other hand, their dedication and sacrifices are arguably extreme. They've forfeited their quality of life.

It's easy to fall into this trap. I fell into it myself when I had a corporate job. It wasn't worth it. The price was too high. My physical health suffered. My mental health suffered. My emotional control eroded. My relationships went sideways. I achieved some of my goals, but my quality of life plummeted.

This problem is more common than you might imagine. Think of the athlete who gives up everything to practice and train, hoping to play professionally. Consider the musician who toils relentlessly to master their craft, hoping to be discovered. Think of the investment banker who puts in 100 hours per week, fueled by coffee and illicit stimulants, hoping to get rich. They might achieve their goals but pay a ruinous price to do so.

Self-discipline is usually discussed in the context of how you'll benefit if you develop it. That's understandable, as it's a skill that'll pay meaningful dividends throughout your life. The part of the discussion usually missing is how to avoid taking self-discipline too far. If your success is overshadowed by regret, it suggests an alarming imbalance.

How to Find a Healthy Balance

There are two things you can do to manage your self-discipline habit. First, review your purpose (for more on this topic, see *Step #3*). Ask yourself why you'd like to be disciplined in this area of your life. Is your purpose realistic? What are your odds of achieving your goal? Given your odds and the sacrifice it'll involve, is your goal reasonable?

For example, imagine that you want to learn to play the guitar. Becoming proficient will require a significant amount of time and effort. It'll require discipline. So, consider what's driving this goal. Do you want to learn to play the guitar because it brings you joy? Or do you aspire to join a world-famous band and become a best-selling musician? Is your goal realistic? Is it reasonable?

The second thing you can do to maintain balance is to

expand your capacity for self-compassion. As we discussed in *Step #1*, you're going to stumble during your journey. It's unavoidable. You'll occasionally make decisions that counter your intentions. You'll give in to your impulses now and then. You must develop the capacity to forgive yourself.

For example, let's say that you commit to playing the guitar for three hours each day. There will undoubtedly be days when you don't feel like putting in that much time. If you can show yourself compassion, you'll be less inclined to drive yourself to extremes. You'll be more willing to recognize the value in occasionally entertaining your impulses rather than maintaining draconian standards that imperil your quality of life.

You'll achieve balance.

It took me a long time to figure out this aspect of self-discipline. I used to equate self-compassion with weakness and lack of commitment. It was a terrible mistake. An error that I now realize imposed an outrageous, needless cost.

When I finally recognized the gravity of showing myself compassion, I discovered that I could better manage my self-discipline habit. I found balance. I abandoned the extremes, reviewed the intentions that fueled my goals, and gave myself latitude. And I experienced a better quality of life in the process.

In my opinion, it's impossible to overstate how crucial this often-ignored aspect of self-discipline is. Without the capacity for self-compassion, pursuing discipline is almost guaranteed to lead to regret and shame.

∼

EXERCISE #16

∼

Pick one goal that you'd like to achieve. Think about the sacrifices you'll need to make to achieve it. Write them down.

Next, consider your reason for pursuing this goal. Why do you want to achieve it? Then, ask yourself whether your goal is realistic.

Lastly, write down three things you can do to maintain a healthy balance between your discipline and present quality of life.

For example, imagine you want to give up all foods containing added sugar. This means giving up your favorite treats and snacks. It means forfeiting sugary drinks. It might involve refusing desserts at birthday parties and other social gatherings.

Now, ask yourself why you want to give up sugar. Is your reason… reasonable?

Consider whether giving up sugar entirely is realistic. Or is it extreme? Can you do it without feeling as though you're sacrificing your current quality of life?

Finally, come up with three ways to give yourself the freedom to indulge occasionally. Here are a few examples:

- Have a cheat day (or cheat meal)
- Use your favorite snack as a reward
- Allow yourself latitude at social gatherings

This freedom tempers your self-discipline habit. It'll help you to maintain balance and avoid extremism. Assuming your goals are reasonable, you'll still achieve them without ruining your present quality of life.

Time required: 20 minutes

THE EFFECT OF LIFESTYLE CHOICES
ON YOUR SELF-DISCIPLINE HABIT

~

❝❝ Self-discipline is only punishment when imposed by someone else. When you discipline yourself, it's not punishment but empowerment.

— LES BROWN

Throughout this book, we've focused on developing and strengthening your self-discipline by following a step-by-step system. This system emphasizes an orderly approach, prioritizing steps like effective goal-setting, purpose clarification, resistance control, and stress management. These and other steps are pivotal to your success.

But your lifestyle choices can also play a vital role. Healthy choices will buttress your new self-discipline habit. Unhealthy choices can severely undermine it.

How Lifestyle Choices Affect Impulse Control

Recall a time when you felt utterly exhausted — physically, mentally, and emotionally. It was probably hard to focus. It wasn't easy to make good decisions. And emotional control was either out the window or on its way. At that moment, your self-control waned, making you more susceptible to your impulses.

Now, recall a time when you felt invigorated. You likely found it easy to focus. You were able to make purposeful decisions that supported your intentions and goals. You had a tight rein on your emotions. At *that* moment, you probably had remarkable self-control.

Many factors influence how exhausted or invigorated you feel throughout each day. The good news is that you control them. You get to make these choices.

Consider your diet. If you consume a lot of refined sugar, you'll likely feel sluggish and irritable as the sugar rush wears off (and it wears off quickly!). Moreover, nutritional deficiencies can lead to fatigue and cognitive impairment even if you avoid sugar.[1] You control this.

Consider the duration and quality of your sleep. Insufficient sleep will leave you exhausted and make you more susceptible to stress and negative emotions.[2] Although it may seem otherwise, you have significant control over your sleep.

Consider alcohol. It does more than affect your balance, slur your speech, and make you do things that your friends will joke about the following day. It can lower your sleep quality, which exposes you to fatigue. Alcohol can indeed induce sleep (who hasn't observed a friend sleeping off a bender?). But the quality of that sleep is usually poor. The crucial thing to note is that you control this.

We're just scratching the surface. Many other lifestyle choices can heavily influence your self-discipline and impulse control. They can affect the level of energy you possess each day. The more exhausted you feel, the more difficult it'll be to keep yourself in check. The more rested you feel, the *easier* it'll be.

The takeaway is that your lifestyle choices are precisely that: choices. You're in control. It may not be easy to make healthy choices. It may be exceptionally tough. But doing so is feasible, especially with support from those who care about you.

"Surfing" Your Urges Without Giving in to Them

Our lifestyle choices usually stem from our urges.[3] For example, we go to bed late because we enjoy watching late-night television. We avoid exercise because we prefer instead to browse the internet. We drink alcohol because we want to feel relaxed and less inhibited. We eat sugary foods because we love the resulting dopamine rush.

Cultivating self-discipline is primarily about resisting these urges. But what if you could acknowledge them in a way that lessens their power? What if you could "ride them out," like surfing a wave, without surrendering to them?

Enter urge surfing.

We often ignore our impulses when we're struggling to remain disciplined. That can be effective, especially if we've trained our brains to respond instinctively to our urges in that manner.

Urge surfing takes the opposite approach. Rather than ignoring our impulses, it entails admitting they exist and addressing them face-on. We don't give in to them. We acknowledge them. When we do so, their power over us recedes like a wave after it peaks.

Here's how it works...

When you experience an urge, stop what you're doing. Accept that it exists. Don't blame yourself. Don't shame yourself. Your desires do not reflect your character. They arise from your routines, vices, and dependencies. It's natural to have them.

Nor do your urges signify actions you must take. You can decide not to take them. These impulses merely reflect how you feel about something in the moment. They are short-lived and will eventually pass.

Unsatisfied urges will cause you to feel unsettled, agitated, and restless. It's okay to have these feelings. It's okay to feel uncomfortable. Remember, your urges are fleeting. They'll pass. You don't have to give in to them.

That's the essence of urge surfing. You don't ignore your urges. You don't suppress them. You grant they exist; you recognize that it's natural to have them; you note that they're transient and will pass in due course.

This removes their power over you. They lose their intensity, like a strong wave that spends its energy and returns to the ocean.

EXERCISE #17

WRITE down every lifestyle choice that might affect your energy levels. Be specific. Here are a few examples you can use to get started:

- I drink alcohol each evening and feel sick the next morning.
- I go to bed too late and feel tired the next day.
- I eat sugary treats throughout the day and feel drowsy after the rush wears off.
- I never exercise and feel perpetually sluggish.

Next, review your list and devise one healthy way to change each habit or routine. For example, you might limit your alcohol consumption to Saturday nights. Or you might choose to go to bed 30 minutes earlier each evening. Or you might commit to skipping your afternoon sugar-laden treat (or replace it with a healthier option).

Finally, monitor how these changes impact your energy levels. Don't be surprised if you find that you have more energy. Note how this affects your ability to control your impulses and stay committed to your intentions.

Time required: 15 minutes

---

1. LaChance, L., & Ramsey, D. (2015). Food, mood, and brain health: implications for the modern clinician. *PubMed, 112*(2), 111–115.
2. Saghir, Z., Syeda, J. N., Muhammad, A. S., & Abdalla, T. H. B. (2018). The amygdala, sleep debt, sleep deprivation, and the emotion of anger: a possible connection? *Cureus.*
3. This isn't always the case, of course, but enough so that we can at least start with this presumption.

FINAL THOUGHTS ON HOW TO LEAD
A DISCIPLINED LIFE

~

Self-discipline can be a perplexing topic. On the one hand, we assume that we can set boundaries, exert self-control, and go the extra mile whenever we wish. We figure our future selves are up to the challenge.

On the other hand, it sometimes seems as though we'll never possess the discipline we need to achieve our goals. It can feel as if the perseverance, fortitude, and grit we require lie just outside our grasp. Consequently, it can feel as though our stories are being written for us rather than *by* us.

The reality is more straightforward.

None of us are born with self-discipline. Yet, each of us can develop it.

Regardless of your vices, past, circumstances, regrets,

and goals, you can decide to be disciplined. Once you choose this destination, you can travel at your own pace. The important thing is that you have a clear, practical roadmap to guide you.

This map should provide step-by-step directions, of course. But it should also highlight the hazards you'll want to avoid during your journey.

How to Lead a Disciplined Life is your roadmap. It gives you the needed directions and highlights the obstacles you'll face. It takes you through each leg of your journey, step by step, offering practical, actionable tips along the way so you'll reach your destination smoothly.

This doesn't mean your trip will be easy. Indeed, you'll encounter roadblocks that challenge your resolve. But if you follow your map, you will make progress. Follow it to the end, and you'll develop the self-discipline you need to achieve your goals.

I guarantee it.

One last note: This journey never truly ends. Life will repeatedly try to whittle away your self-discipline habit. So, I encourage you to return to this book whenever you need a refresher. You don't have to reread the entire book. Just revisit the section of your "map" that addresses the road-blocks you're facing.

Enjoy this adventure, confident that the time and effort you invest today will pay remarkable dividends for the rest of your life.

DID YOU ENJOY READING HOW TO LEAD A DISCIPLINED LIFE?

⁓

We've spent quite a bit of time together in this book. Thank you for that. I appreciate your willingness to take this journey with me, and I hope you found it to be a rewarding experience.

I want to ask you for a small favor. If you enjoyed reading *How to Lead a Disciplined Life*, would you leave a short review for the book on Amazon? A sentence or two about something that helped you would mean the world to me.

Potential readers want to hear from folks like yourself who have read the book. Your review will encourage them to give the book a try.

One last note: I usually release new books at a steep discount. It's my way of thanking readers for their time and trust.

If you'd like to be notified when this happens, be sure to join my mailing list. You'll immediately receive my 40-page PDF ebook titled *Catapult Your Productivity! The Top 10 Habits You Must Develop to Get More Things Done.*

You can join my list at the following address:

http://artofproductivity.com/free-gift/

I'll also send you my best productivity, time management, and self-improvement advice via my email newsletter. You'll receive tips and tactics on beating procrastination, creating morning routines, avoiding burnout, and developing razor-sharp focus, along with many other productivity hacks!

If you have questions or want to share a tip, technique, or mind hack that has made a positive difference in your life, please get in touch with me at damon@artofproductivity.com. I'd love to hear about it!

Until next time,

Damon Zahariades
http://artofproductivity.com

ABOUT THE AUTHOR

Damon Zahariades is a corporate refugee who endured years of unnecessary meetings, drive-by chats with coworkers, and a distraction-laden work environment before striking out on his own. Today, in addition to writing a growing catalog of time management and productivity books, he's the showrunner for the productivity blog <u>ArtofProductivity.com</u>.

In his spare time, he enjoys playing chess, poker, and the occasional video game with friends. And he continues to promise himself that he'll start playing the guitar again.

Damon lives in Southern California with his beautiful, supportive wife and their affectionate, quirky, and sometimes mischievous dog. He's looking wistfully at his 50th birthday in the rearview mirror.

OTHER BOOKS BY DAMON ZAHARIADES

∽

The Mental Toughness Handbook

The Procrastination Cure

To-Do List Formula

The Time Management Solution

80/20 Your Life!

The Time Chunking Method

How to Make Better Decisions

The Art of Living Well series

The Art Of Saying NO

The Art of Letting GO

The Art of Finding FLOW

The 30-Day Productivity Boost series

The 30-Day Productivity Plan - VOLUME I

The 30-Day Productivity Plan - VOLUME II

Self-Help Books for Busy People series

Small Habits Revolution

The Joy Of Imperfection

The P.R.I.M.E.R. Goal Setting Method

Improve Your Focus and Mental Discipline series

Fast Focus

Morning Makeover

Digital Detox

Visit ArtofProductivity.com for a complete list of titles and summaries. All titles are available for purchase at ArtofProductivity.com/Amazon.

Made in the USA
Las Vegas, NV
12 November 2024

5310497f-d6ce-4c57-bed9-6311398bb8bcR01